Latin American Experiments
in Neoconservative Economics

Latin American Experiments in Neoconservative Economics

ALEJANDRO FOXLEY

University of California Press

Berkeley, Los Angeles, London

University of California Press
Berkeley and Los Angeles, California

University of California Press, Ltd.
London, England
©1983 by The Regents
of the University of California
Printed in the United States of America

1   2   3   4   5   6   7   8   9

Library of Congress Cataloging
in Publication Data

Foxley, Alejandro.
    Latin American experiments in neoconserva-
tive economics.

    Includes index.
    1. South America—Economic policy. 2. Eco-
nomic stabilization—South America. 3. Monetary
policy—South America. 4. Economics—South
America. 5. Chile—Economic policy. I. Title.
HC165.F675   1983   338.98   82-20252
ISBN 0-520-04807-5

Contents

PART ONE Radical Conservative
Economics in Practice

Tables and Figures

Tables

Figures

Abbreviations

CEBRAP — Centro Brasileiro de Analise e Planemento
(Brazilian Center for Planning, Brazil)

CEDES — Centro de Estudios del Estado y Sociedad
(Center for the Study of State and Society, Argentina)

CEPAL — Comission Económica para América Latina de Naciones Unidas
(U.N. Economic Commission for Latin America)

CIDE — Centro de Investigación y Docencia Económica
(Center for Research and Teaching in Economics, Mexico)

CIEPLAN — Corporación de Investigaciones Económicas para Latinoamérica
(Center for Latin American Economic Research, Chile)

CIESU — Centro de Investigaciones Socilógicas del Uruguay
(Center for Sociological Research, Uruguay)

CINVE — Centro de Investigaciones Económicas
(Center for Economic Research, Uruguay)

CONAF — Corporación Nacional Forestal
(National Forestry Corporation, Chile)

CORA — Corporación de Reforma Agraria
(Land Reform Corporation, Chile)

CORFO — Corporación de Fomento
(Development Corporation, Chile)

IDES — Instituto de Desarrollo
(Development Institute, Argentina)

INE — Instituto Nacional de Estadísticas
(Institute of National Statistics, Chile)

xi

ODENA   Oficina de Normalización Agrícola
(Office of Agricultural Normalization, Chile)

ODEPLAN   Oficina de Planificación Nacional
(National Planning Office, Chile)

PEM   Programa de Empleo Mínimo
(Minimum Employment Program, Chile)

PREALC   Programa Regional del Empleo para América
Latina de Naciones Unidas
*(UN Regional Employment Program for Latin
America, Santiago, Chile)*

SOFOFA   Sociedad de Fomento Fabril
(Association of Manufacturers, Chile)

Preface

THIS book represents an effort to understand the nature and effects of the new type of radical economic orthodoxy that has been espoused by authoritarian governments in Latin America during the sixties and seventies. These economic experiments continue to be applied during the early eighties in Argentina, Chile, Uruguay, and, to a lesser extent, in Brazil.

These experiments are carried on in the context of deep revolutionary changes in a neoconservative and strongly authoritarian direction. As such, they have a deep impact in society. Radical economic changes and political repression go hand in hand. Thus, it is not easy to totally dissociate economic performance from prevailing political conditions. The task is particularly difficult when one has been and is a close witness to these changes.

Because of this, the reader deserves a word of warning about where the author stands. As a human being and as an economist I profess some beliefs that I cannot pretend are absent from what follows. These are a deep commitment to democratic values and institutions and a marked preference for a more rather than a less egalitarian society. It is not surprising then that I take a critical view of current neoconservative, authoritarian experiences.

Having said this, I must add that I have made a serious effort to undertake an objective, scholarly appraisal of these neoconservative experiments. Obviously, the reader will be the final judge on whether or not I have succeeded. But it is important to stress that although in evaluating economic policies one should judge them on their own merits, it is also true that their overall impact on the economy and on society cannot be ignored. This is particularly true when dealing with radical, revolutionary changes as those which have been undertaken by authoritarian governments in Latin America.

This book reflects the various avenues of research that I have pursued in the last few years, attempting to grasp the full meaning of the neoconservative experiments in Latin America. This effort has been a part of a joint research project with colleagues at the Center for the Study of State and Society in Argentina (CEDES), the Brazilian Center for Planning (CEBRAP), and the Center for Economic Research (CINVE) and the Center for Sociological Research (CIESU) in Uruguay. A complete, interdisciplinary, and comparative treatment of some of the issues that are touched upon here and many other significant topics must await completion of this joint project.

My own research has been done as part of the research program at the Center for Latin American Economic Research (CIEPLAN) in Santiago, Chile. Valuable financial support has been received at various stages from the Ford Foundation, the Swedish Agency for Research Cooperation, the International Labor Office, the Latin American Social Sciences Council, and the International Development Research Corporation, Canada. Support from the last has been essential for pursuing partially researched topics to the synthesis attempted in this book. The University of California at Berkeley invited me to lecture in the winter quarter of 1981 and allowed me to concentrate on drafting this manuscript. My deep appreciation goes to the Center for Latin American Studies at Berkeley, particularly to its chairman, David Collier, who was an enthusiastic supporter at a critical stage; and also to the Department of Economics.

My thanks are also due to Lovell Jarvis, Emilio Klein, Felipe Morandé, Ernesto Tironi, Víctor Tokman, Andrés Solimano,

Pilar Vergara and my colleagues in CIEPLAN. All were patient in reading the manuscript and giving me valuable suggestions, but, as usual, responsibility remains with the author. Paulina Cortés, and Gabriela and Victoria Nathan efficiently typed several versions of the manuscript, and I am grateful for their collaboration. The intellectual environment at CIEPLAN was essential for the completion of this book. I benefited from various pieces of research undertaken by colleagues, as acknowledged in the text. But above all, I was stimulated by many collective discussions on the topics covered in this book. A final word of appreciation goes to my family for their infinite patience while this book was being written. In some sense, it also belongs to them.

Introduction

THIS book deals with neoconservative economic policies in contemporary Latin America. As a result of various factors that will be examined below, a new phenomenon has been present in Latin America—the marriage of monetarist views concerning economic stabilization with radical conservative approaches. Both ingredients have been present in varying degrees in the economic programs put into practice by the governments of Chile after 1973, Uruguay after 1974, and Argentina after 1976.

These experiments in economic policymaking have been undertaken by strong military governments. By repressing dissidence and not allowing the normal expression of public opinion as is common in a democracy, the authoritarian regimes have sought to impose a new discipline on the social body, one that is supposed to rectify previous trends and disorders. Economic policies play a key role in the process.

These military governments inherited an economy suffering from three-digit inflation and a critical situation in the balance of payments. The normal supply of goods and services was disrupted, labor absenteeism was high, and the economy was believed to be approaching a critical point. At the same time, political mobilization and social conflict were on the rise. Governments presiding over these processes were increasingly unable to bring the situation under control. Finally, the regimes collapsed, and the military took over.

The initial task in the economic sphere for the new governments was to bring inflation under control, eliminate the deficit in the balance of payments, and restore normal conditions in

1

the production and distribution of goods and services. To do this, an economic stabilization program was introduced, which proposed to reduce government expenditures, to decrease the growth of money supply, to sharply devalue domestic currency, and to deregulate most prices so that the market would play the main role in resource allocation. Inflation was diagnosed as basically a monetary phenomenon, hence the key role assigned to monetary policy within the stabilization program.

Monetarism was not entirely new in Latin America. Monetarist stabilization programs had been enforced in several countries in the late 1950s. But the new programs in the 1970s put a stronger emphasis on long-term structural and institutional changes. Opening up the economy to world trade and capital flows, developing a private financial sector, and drastically reducing the role of government in the economy were central elements in the new programs.

At the same time, deep institutional changes were put into practice that affected labor legislation, the way social services were provided, and decision-making mechanisms in the economy. These changes were directed toward "disciplining" economic agents through free market forces, decentralizing decision processes, and transferring as many functions as possible (including the provision of social services) to the private sector. The withdrawal of the state from the economic sphere was accompanied by the centralization of political power in the state. The military junta exerted the executive and legislative powers and defined new rules of the game for economic agents. Labor organizations were either suppressed or their activities severely curtailed. Collective bargaining was suspended until new labor legislation redefined the role and place of workers' organizations within the new economic institutions to be developed by the government. Business groups continued to participate and influence economic decision making. Emergency powers for the government allowed it to suppress political parties and centrally to control social organizations, the educational system, and the media.

However, all of these were considered to be just emergency measures. If the authoritarian government was going to be more than a transitional government, it needed a more ambitious and permanent project for transforming the economy and society. Previous threats to existing institutions from the Left had created the conditions for a reaction from the Right. Neoconservative intellectuals and orthodox technocrats provided such a project. Given the appropriate conditions and circumstances, the governments incorporated at least part of the neoconservative project in their programs.

The degree to which this happened depended on the ideology of the military, on the nature of the alliance supporting the government, and on the degree of autonomy of the latter vis-à-vis civil society, which again was a function of the intensity of the previous threats from the Left as perceived by the new ruling powers.

Another factor that influenced the extent to which the long-term radical project was introduced was the relative success of the short-term stabilization goals. If the economic program was not successful in performing the basic tasks of reducing the rate of inflation, balancing the external accounts, and "normalizing" productive activities, the long-term structural transformations tended to be deemphasized. This seemed to have been the fate of the post-1974 economic program in Uruguay and of the stabilization program in Argentina after the 1976 coup.

On the other hand, when a reasonable degree of success was achieved in the stabilization goals at a time when the military government was still strong and no serious cleavages had eroded its support in the business groups, the economic program evolved toward its more radical version. A drastic privatization of most functions, economic and otherwise, of the government was proposed and gradually implemented. This included privatization of public enterprises; social services such as social security, health, and education; and utilities and the infrastructure (e.g., the postal service, port administration, electricity, transport, communications, and even road administration).

The basic philosophy behind such a program is the radical conservative credo that decentralizing economic decision making will be best achieved when most decisions are made by individuals in market-type situations—considered superior to other forms of decision making. Of course, the peculiar characteristic of the process in recent Latin American experience is that this kind of radical conservative economic program is proposed and gradually implemented in an environment where political decision making is highly centralized and authoritarian.

The most clear case of a monetarist stabilization program evolving toward a drastic and radical conservative program is found in the Chilean experience after 1973, although the examples of Argentina and Uruguay in the 1970s also represent a more radical set of right-wing economic policies than previously experienced in those countries. But the pure case is undoubtedly provided by the so-called "Chicago experiment" in Chile.

This book attempts to provide an intelligible, although preliminary and not necessarily complete, picture of the phenomenon we have been talking about. Since it consists in the blend of two separable components—radical conservative economics in practice and monetarist stabilization policies—we will try to deal with them in a sequential manner, although both are inextricably bound together. Given the author's familiarity with the Chilean case, what follows will be heavily influenced by this particular case, although an attempt has been made to generalize whenever the argument and evidence seem to grant it.

The major questions that will be addressed here reflect the

two-dimensional nature of current neoconservative economic programs in Latin America. The first set of questions, to be dealt with in Part 1 of this book, refers to the process of radicalization of monetarist economic policies. Why is it that economic stabilization policies became more radical in the 1970s and 1980s when compared with equivalent experiences in the 1950s and 1960s? What factors explain this? This question is examined in Chapters 1 and 2. A second preoccupation will be the nature of radical conservative economics in Latin America. This issue is examined in Chapters 3 and 4. In particular, we are interested in exploring the relationship between short-term stabilization policies and long-term structural and institutional changes, and the role of ideology in providing the bridge between the two. This will be done by examining in detail the case of Chile, which is the clearest example of the phenomenon.

In Part 2, we will try to answer a different set of questions. They are narrower, more technical questions. How does this monetarist-neoconservative approach perform strictly as a stabilization instrument? We will evaluate the results of the policies and provide some preliminary interpretation of the causal factors behind the results. We will also evaluate the economic adjustment processes and their probable effects when monetarism in its peculiar Latin American version is applied in order to stabilize the economy under conditions where political behavior is controlled by an authoritarian government.

In Chapter 5 we identify the theoretical approaches behind the stabilization policies. Chapter 6 deals with the economics of stabilization policies and stagflation and reviews the relevant literature. Chapter 7 discusses the impact of various stabilization instruments on output and employment levels, trying to explain the persistent stagflation that accompanies the stabilization effort. In Chapter 8, we take up the main themes that have emerged and suggest some tentative conclusions.

The method we have chosen in order to explore the questions in Part 1 is closer to that of political economy than that of conventional economics. This is because economic policies that are part of a broader political process of deep transformation in society cannot be understood by economic analysis alone. It is in the interaction of economic and political forces and processes that we will find the key to understanding why certain economic policies are chosen and why they produce certain results. In Part 2, we turn to more conventional economic approaches in order to evaluate the results of the stabilization policies.

After finishing research for this book, I was firmly convinced that the piecemeal approach of evaluating an economic program so frequently advocated by monetarist-conservatives (i.e., examining each economic instrument separately and evaluating whether or not each policy action was "efficient") is insufficient and may be seriously misleading. It will certainly be misleading and incomplete when Latin American experiments with radical conservative economics are examined, given the all-encompassing nature of the phenomenon.

We are aware of the risks of adventuring in paths not often covered by conventional economics. The method followed implies an explicit choice of a broader treatment of the multitude of issues that emerge from an exploratory study such as this one. This choice is made at the expense of a more formal (in the sense of economic modeling) or detailed treatment of the issues.

This method was forced upon us not only because of the nature of the subject matter but also because empirical research is patently insufficient. Given the limitations, this study must be considered exploratory. It is our hope that it will provide the stimulus for others to pursue the many avenues of research that suggest themselves from the pages that follow.

PART ONE

Radical
Conservative
Economics
In Practice

1

Monetarism, Structuralism, and All That

Rᴀᴅɪᴄᴀʟ conservative economics in Latin America is connected in its origins with monetarist ideas about economic stabilization that have been present in several Latin American countries since the 1950s. Inflation has been such a dominant economic phenomenon in the past decades that it is not surprising that the main economic debates have centered around this problem.

Although we will cover familiar material, we find it useful to start our discussion of current economic policies by briefly referring to the old monetarist-structuralist debate in Latin America. We do this not for the sake of reviving an old debate but in order to understand the relation between current neoconservative economic policies and those two important currents of economic thought that dominated the scene for more than two decades. First, I will briefly review the ideas behind monetarism and structuralism and what happened when they were put into practice. Then, I will characterize the new economic policies in the 1970s and 1980s, using as a reference point the types of policies that were applied in the 1950s and 1960s.

Historical Perspective

A Latin American perspective on the problem of inflation and economic stabilization must begin by referring to the two main currents that have influenced the thinking about inflation since the 1950s: structuralism and monetarism. The interest is not purely academic. In fact, as will be shown further on, both schools of thought have deeply influenced the design and application of stabilization policies in Latin America. By contrasting theoretical conception and historical experience, we can learn something about the effects of policies conceived under radically different assumptions.

The subject is of interest not only to Latin Americans. The so-called "New inflation" in developed countries and the subsequent discussion as to why the traditional monetary-fiscal approach has failed in bringing it down within a reasonable period of time have resulted in increasing attention to the structural factors behind the inflationary forces prevailing in developed countries today.[1] The parallel with debates in Latin America in the late 1950s and 1960s is striking, as Hirschman and Diamand have pointed out.[2]

The structural approach asserts that the roots of inflation are imbedded in the economic structure. This is characterized in developing countries by resource immobility, market segmentation, and disequilibria between sectoral demands and supplies. As growth proceeds, the economy is prone to develop extended bottlenecks since the changes in demand associated

1. See F. Modigliani, "The Monetarist Controversy or Should We Forsake Stabilization Policies?" *American Economic Review,* March 1977.
2. A. Hirschman, "The Social and Political Matrix of Inflation: Elaborations on the Latin American Experience," *Brookings Project on the Politics and Sociology of Global Inflation,* Oct. 1978 (mimeo); M. Diamand, "Toward a Change in the Economic Paradigm Through the Experience of Developing Countries," *Journal of Development Economics* 5(1) (March 1978).

with higher income levels are not followed by an adequate supply response.

A characterization of the main bottlenecks includes the supply of food products, the availability of foreign exchange, the rigidity in the tax and expenditure structure of the government, the inability to raise enough internal savings, and the supply of various intermediate inputs, whose relative scarcity varies depending on the country's resource base and in some cases on the level of development achieved.[3] We refer to inputs like fuels, fertilizers, transport facilities, credit availability, etc.

According to the structural view, a stabilization policy that does not recognize the existence of such bottlenecks is doomed to failure. It may reduce one disequilibrium (the rate of inflation) but at the expense of creating other disequilibria: excess capacity, unemployment, and concentration of income and wealth. The main thrust of a structuralist stabilization policy then lies in doing away with the bottlenecks that are forcing the economy to go through inflationary cycles. Almost by definition, this is basically a long-run policy since structural disequilibria can be eliminated only by a reallocation of investments. Thus, controlling inflation is necessarily a gradual process.

The structuralist view of stabilization is not only gradual and rather long run, but it is also part of a reformist or, in some historical cases, revolutionary process of change. According to this view, deep institutional reforms are needed if bottlenecks are to disappear. Land reform, tax changes, and state intervention in various areas of economic activity are required if the

3. See C. H. Kirkpatrick and F. I. Nixson, "The Origins of Inflation in Less-Developed Countries: A Selective Review," in M. Parkin and G. Zis, eds., *Inflation in Open Economics* (Manchester University Press, 1976); O. Sunkel, "La inflación chilena: Un enfoque heterodoxo," *El Trimestre Económico*, Oct. 1958; A. Pinto, *La inflación, raíces estructurales,* Serie de Lecturas El Trimestre Económico No. 3, Mexico (1973).

roots of inflation are to be eliminated. All these changes would negatively affect the income of those who control the scarce resources where bottlenecks originate: the owners of land and those who control key raw materials or exports. Resources extracted from these sectors would be channeled to the state. They would provide the basis for sustaining productivity increases and income redistribution in the lagging, poorer segments of the economy. Structural reforms would produce a progressive income redistribution in the long run.

By contrast, the monetarist view is generally thought to be short term and favoring a rapid control of inflation. In a somewhat ambiguous but revealing statement, a monetarist has asserted that "the monetarist is a structuralist in a hurry."[4] According to this view, inflation is negative for efficient growth. It also produces negative income distribution effects mainly through the presumably regressive "inflation tax."[5] Thus, the monetarist approach to stabilization is consistent with a strong preference for zero inflation. The shorter the period before this goal is achieved, the better. In this sense, a "shock treatment" approach to stabilization is more desirable than a gradual adjustment to equilibrium.

The monetarist approach is usually focused on the use of a few policy instruments: control of money supply, reduction of the government deficit, exchange rate devaluation, freeing of prices, and eliminating subsidies. These instruments are assumed to produce neutral distributive effects as a consequence of the application of a uniform "rule" for all economic agents: the working of a free price system.

These were roughly—and in a very summary form indeed—the views on stabilization prevalent in the 1950s and

4. The quotation is from Roberto Campos.
5. See D. Laidler and J. Parkin, "Inflation: A Survey," *Economic Journal,* Dec. 1975.

1960s in Latin America and which were tested in various countries and political circumstances. The late 1950s saw the application of monetarist programs in several countries, including Chile in 1956–1958, Argentina in 1959–1962, Bolivia in 1956, Peru in 1959, and Uruguay in 1959–1962. The results of these experiences have been compared and described by many authors.[6] The policies applied followed rather closely the orthodox package: monetary and credit contraction, reduction in public expenditures, a fall in real wages, exchange rate devaluation, increases in utility rates, and elimination of subsidies and price controls.

The short-run results of the policies were judged to be, on the whole, unsuccessful. While typically the inflation rates decreased for a short period, production at the same time fell, unemployment went up rapidly, and the income share of wage earners deteriorated.

The structuralists' turn in applying their policies came in the 1960s and early 1970s. A good example is the stabilization program during the Frei administration in Chile.[7] The idea was to stabilize the economy gradually and at the same time undertake those long-term reforms needed to overcome the basic bottlenecks in the agricultural, external, and fiscal sectors. At the same time, income redistribution was an explicit policy objective. This was to be achieved by (1) land reform, (2) the reorientation of public developmental programs toward small producers, (3) increasing expenditures in housing, health, and

6. For comparative reviews of the policies see CIDE, "Papel de las políticas de estabilización," *Economía de América Latina* (Mexico), Sept. 1978; O. Sunkel, "El fracaso de las políticas de estabilización en el contexto del proceso de desarrollo latinoamericano," *El Trimestre Económico,* Oct. 1963; and R. Thorp, "Inflation and the Financing of Economic Development," in K. Griffin, ed., *Financing Development in Latin America* (Macmillan, 1971).

7. R. Ffrench-Davis, *Políticas económicas en Chile 1952–1970* (Ediciones Nueva Universidad, Santiago, 1973).

education, and (4) generous wage policies. After six years, the results show an inflation rate stabilizing around 30% a year, moderate growth , and significant gains in labor participation in the national income.[8]

The relatively high rate of inflation at the end of the reformist structuralist experiment was only an external sign of a problem that is inherent in this type of stabilization package: in order to be successful, it needs to advance consistently in three fronts: price stability, structural reforms, and income redistribution. The balance is precarious. It may easily be disrupted by dissatisfied pressure groups (organized labor in the case that we are examining). If, for example, wage increases get out of line, this is bound to be reflected in a higher rate of inflation than was originally programed.

Besides the monetarist and structuralist experience, one finds another type of stabilization policy in the populist regimes in Latin America. These programs typically apply extended price controls while at the same time expanding wages, government expenditures, and the money supply. The Perón administrations in Argentina (1946–1952 and 1973–1976) and the Radical Party government (1963–1966) are adequate illustrations of populist policies.[9] As can be easily predicted, detailed price controls and large increases in expenditures make up for an inconsistent policy package. After a brief initial success in redistributing income toward wage earners and moderating the rate of inflation, the imbalances generated by the policy result in accelerating inflation and a regression in the initial distributive gains.

---

8. The share of salaried income, according to National Accounts estimates, increased from 44.8% in 1964 to 52.3% in 1970; see ODEPLAN, *Cuentas Nacionales de Chile* (Santiago, n.d.).

9. See A. Canitrot, "La experiencia populista de redistribución de ingresos," *Desarrollo Económico* 15(59) (1975).

The "New" Stabilization Policies of the 1970s and 1980s

The 1970s witnessed a return to prestructuralist policies, with some important new features as will be described later. The failure of populist experiences brought about not only a full reversal in economic policies but the breakdown of the democratic political system in many countries. Since we will discuss this in Chapter 2, we will only note here that one factor in this breakdown was "the low propensity of policymakers to defer to normal economic constraints" when implementing stabilization policies during the populist experiences. [10] This was one of the elements leading to high inflation, extended bottlenecks in production, scarcity of basic goods, and losses in real income for almost all groups in society. The result was that wrong economic policies reinforced the political instability of the regimes and contributed to their replacement by authoritarian military governments.

As a reaction to the previous experience, these governments chose to apply strictly orthodox policies as they were heavily influenced by the modern monetarist approach. At the same time they reversed the previous trend toward increased economic and political participation by excluding workers and workers' organizations from decision-making mechanisms both in the political and economic spheres.

It would seem on the surface that as far as stabilization policies are concerned, the process had come full circle, back to the approach to stabilization of the late 1950s. Although, in fact, many of the policies being applied today in several Latin Amer-

---

10. The quotation is from A. Hirschman, "The Turn to Authoritarianism in Latin America and the Search for Its Economic Determinants," in D. Collier, ed., *The New Authoritarianism in Latin America* (Princeton University Press, 1979).

ican countries bear strong resemblance to those of the 1950s, there are at least two new components that must be taken into account.

One is a political component: orthodox policies are being applied today by authoritarian military governments. This seems to solve what the monetarists saw as the reason for the previous failures: the premature reversal of the policies, caused by the adverse reaction of the social groups most affected, mainly the workers; and the "partial" application of the package.

Obviously, an authoritarian government should have no problem in "disciplining" its workers and in controlling the political and social environment in such a way that a sustained application of a consistent stabilization policy is possible. Thus, authoritarianism is presented almost as a requisite for the success of the orthodox economic policies.

The second new element in the orthodox policies of the 1970s was their strong long-term component. Monetarism is usually associated with short-term adjustment policies, and their degree of success is judged accordingly. In their present version in Latin America, the orthodox policies put a heavy emphasis on changing the more fundamental ways in which the economy works. In a curious parallel to structuralist thinking, inflation is increasingly viewed as the result of an economic system that does not work.

Solving the problem of inflation requires a radical transformation of the economy. This involves such "structural" changes as reducing the size of the public sector, reorienting the surplus to the private capitalist sector, creating private capital markets, opening up the economy to free trade, and redefining the participation of private enterprise vis-à-vis labor organizations in decision-making mechanisms. Thus, the original problem, inflation, is "escalated" to a generalized malfunctioning of the economy.

In this sense, it could be argued that the new stabilization policies in Latin America are a form of structuralism using orthodox instruments. Obviously the direction, content, social support, and alliances behind it are entirely different. To give one example: while the structuralism of the sixties was incorporating the poorer masses of workers and peasants to the benefits of the system, the main aim of the new structuralism of the 1970s was to "modernize" the economy by incorporating it into the world economy and by favoring free market, pro-business policies. If this required excluding workers from political and economic participation, then this was a task that had to be undertaken.

In short, the two new elements in the recent stabilization policies in Latin America seem to be (1) the political framework within which they are applied (authoritarianism), and (2) the heavy emphasis on a long-term transformation of the economy as a condition for price stability.

2

The Turn Toward
Radical Economic Policies

THE new stabilization policies of the 1970s in Latin America were characterized by being applied by authoritarian military governments that emphasized a deep transformation of the economy and social and political institutions in order to solve the economic problems, inflation being the one given the highest priority.

In this chapter, we will explore some of the factors that may explain these changes. The changes are twofold. One is an initial turn toward economic orthodoxy, not necessarily a radical one, that accompanied the change in political regime. The existence of large disequilibria in most markets accentuated by ill-conceived populist policies provided a fertile ground for a reactive approach to economic policy that almost necessarily reflected a higher degree of orthodoxy. This entailed an enlarged role for the market, a higher priority for fiscal discipline, and a move toward the elimination of restrictions on foreign trade.

But this was not the only change. If a comparison is made of economic stabilization policies by right-wing military regimes in the 1960s and the 1970s, one will observe a noticeable radicalization in the policies of these regimes in an orthodox and conservative direction. How can this turn toward more radical policies be explained?

First I will deal with the conditions for the emergence of right-wing authoritarian regimes and hence of orthodox policies and then enumerate the factors behind the radicalization of economic policies in the 1970s and 1980s. Then I will illustrate the mild, rather heterodox, policies of the 1960s by describing some features of Brazilian policies. A third section picks up the previous themes in an attempt to provide a reasonable hypothesis as to why the economic policies evolved in the 1970s in a more radical conservative direction. Finally, I will deal with the way changes in the international economy influenced these events.

Change in Political Regime

There is widespread agreement that no single cause can explain the change in political regime and in economic policies that several Latin American countries have undergone since the 1960s. The turn toward political authoritarianism and economic orthodoxy began with Brazil in 1964 and was followed by Argentina in 1966. It received new impetus in the 1970s with Chile, Uruguay, and again with Argentina, which in 1976 initiated a new phase of political and economic changes in a conservative direction under an authoritarian regime.[1]

Recent literature that explores the origin of political authoritarianism stresses a mixture of economic and political factors behind the change in regime. A slowing down of economic growth accompanied by increased inflation and economic instability leads to a crisis of confidence in the economic system both by key domestic actors (workers, businessmen) as well as

1. For an illuminating analysis of this phenomenon, see G. O'Donnell, *Modernization and Bureaucratic Authoritarianism* (Institute of International Studies, University of California, Berkeley, 1973); J. Linz and A. Stepan, eds., *The Breakdown of Democratic Regimes in Latin America* (Johns Hopkins University Press, 1978); and D. Collier, ed., *The New Authoritarianism in Latin America* (Princeton University Press, 1979).

by foreign investors. To the extent that the countries choose to pursue and perhaps accentuate the same economic policies that led to the slowdown, the crisis is aggravated. Political factors are also present. The mobilization of popular groups and the strength of labor organizations create a pervading feeling of threat to business groups and eventually to the military as well. An open, competitive political system allows these conflicting forces to clash until a generalized political stalemate and crisis develop.[2]

Conditions are ripe then for a regime, a coalition, or a policy change or for all of them to occur simultaneously, in which case the authoritarian regime emerges. The new regime represents a new coalition of the military and the more internationalized sector of the business community. It also represents a new approach to economic policies as a response to the inherited economic crisis. The questions that now arise are why this economic crisis developed and what were the factors behind it. We shall now explore these in more detail.

It is no mystery that import substitution industrialization (ISI) had run into trouble by the mid-1960s in those countries in Latin America that had most consistently followed these policies in the postwar period. As Hirschman has convincingly argued, the problem was not so much that of a supposed exhaustion of ISI but rather that the mechanisms used to promote it had run their course and were proving to be an expensive and inefficient way of pushing ISI strategies.[3]

Relative prices had been extensively used as a means of financing industrialization in Latin America. High protection for industry vis-à-vis agriculture, an overvalued domestic cur-

2. D. Collier, "The Bureaucratic-Authoritarian Model: Synthesis and Priorities for Future Research," and R. Kaufman, "Industrial Change and Authoritarian Rule in Latin America," both in Collier, *New Authoritarianism*.

3. A. Hirschman, "The Political Economy of Import-Substituting Industrialization in Latin America," in his *A Bias for Hope* (Yale University Press, 1971).

rency, and import controls made it possible to transfer resources away from the primary sectors to manufacturing. The policies led to periodic balance of payments problems, and inflation became a permanent feature. Through inflationary public expenditures the government was able to take command over resources without resorting to taxation. These resources were then used to finance industrial projects or the provision of infrastructure and social services required by the rapid process of industrialization.

As balance of payments problems become more recurrent, thus preventing the economy from fully using its productive capacity, inflation accelerates. In the face of slower growth and higher inflation, redistributive problems acquire enhanced importance. Antagonistic and mutually inconsistent redistributive objectives by various social groups substitute for the less conflictive global development goals. Whatever one group is going to gain, another one must lose. The economy enters more and more into a zero-sum situation where the various social and economic groups perceive the others as a treat. The political system is strained, and social conflict escalates.[4]

At this point a revision of conventional policies was urgently needed in order to increase efficiency, stimulate growth, reduce economic instability, and enhance the possibilities of an equitable distribution of income. A more significant use of market signals as resource allocation criteria, a realistic exchange rate that would allow balanced external accounts, and a more consistent effort toward export growth were obviously needed, as well as doses of fiscal and monetary restraint on the part of government.

A few countries in Latin America in the 1960s like Colombia and Venezuela were able to move in the required direction without changes in their political system. Chile initiated that

4. A. Hirschman, "The Turn to Authoritarianism in Latin America and the Search for Its Economic Determinants," in Collier, *New Authoritarianism*.

process under the Frei administration, but it was not continued under Allende. Other countries like Brazil and Argentina suffered a breakdown of the political regime instead and embarked on what was at the time a profound revision of economic policies. It was thought that orthodox stabilization measures were required in order to solve the economic problems.

In sum, in the 1960s several countries in Latin America were facing severe economic problems and social and political tensions. These phenomena were not as serious as they were to become in the 1970s. Even so, partly as a result of economic problems and partly out of a political crisis, some countries like Brazil in 1964 and Argentina in 1960, after a military coup, attempted to turn their economic policies toward orthodoxy. The Brazilian experiment lasted only three years and evolved by 1967 toward a mixed package with strong heterodox components. The Argentinian stabilization policy of 1967 was never a case of pure orthodoxy but a mild blend of partial orthodoxy and "desarrollismo." By contrast, similarly authoritarian governments in Chile after 1973, Uruguay after 1974, and Argentina after 1976 followed a more radical course in their policies.

We believe that this is related to four concurrent factors. One was the existence of a much larger disequilibrium in the economy when the new experiments were initiated in the 1970s as compared with the 1960s. Second was the presence of a deeper, more extended political crisis than had been the case in the 1960s. Third was that the degree of threat posed by the populist or socialist coalition that anteceded the military regimes in the 1970s was perceived as being much greater than previously. The fourth originates in the changes that were occurring in the international economy.

It is our contention that in the 1970s most of these factors worked in the direction of reinforcing the feeling of the military that a very serious emergency was being faced and that it required tough solutions. Considerations about the cost of the policies in terms of output losses, unemployment, or regressive social impact became secondary.

Given this climate, it is not surprising that a more radical course was followed particularly when one compares equivalent cases in the 1960s, such as the Brazilian policies after 1964 or the economic stabilization scheme of Argentina between 1967 and 1970.

In contrast to the more radical versions of the 1970s, the 1960s policies look more pragmatic. They seem to have been less influenced by ideological fervor and adjusted more flexibly to the particular conditions or constraints faced by the economies at the time. At the same time, the policy design was more responsive to possible negative side effects of the policies such as recessionary tendencies. Before returning to the more recent cases, we shall illustrate this argument by drawing on the Brazilian economic policies after 1964.

Brazilian Policies
After 1964 Revisited

Brazilian economic policies after the military coup of 1964 represented a turn toward orthodoxy.[5] Reductions in the fiscal deficit, in the expansion of money supply, and in real wages became a high priority, as well as the elimination of extended subsidies and nonmarket restrictions to trade. A gradual reduction of external tariffs was part of the orthodox

5. See A. Foxley, "Stabilization Policies and Stagflation: The Cases of Brazil and Chile," in A. Foxley and L. Whitehead, eds., *Economic Stabilization in Latin America: Political Dimensions* (Pergamon, 1980). Detailed references to studies on Brazilian economic policies, on which my own comparative study was based, are given in Foxley's article.

policy package, as well as a liberalization of regulations affecting foreign investment. However, from the beginning the stabilization policy had some nonorthodox components. Price controls and credit incentives were used in order to curb inflationary pressures. The government took an active role in order to sustain an acceptable level of economic activity. Public investment was used as a countercyclical instrument. Opening up to trade—a typical component of orthodox economic programs—was pursued in a gradual manner so that high unemployment would be avoided. Even monetary and fiscal policy, after a first phase that lasted up to 1967, became mildly expansionary. This proved to be consistent with a reduction in the rate of inflation and high gross domestic product (GDP) growth rates.

Heterodox components in Brazilian policies reflected an early recognition of some structural constraints that were present in the Brazilian economy. Adapting the policies to these constraints was essential to the success of the policies. Let us illustrate this with two examples: trade policies and investment policy.

The structural constraint affecting the external sector was the low relative importance of external vis-à-vis domestic demand. The constraint affecting the level of economic activity was the traditionally high share of total investment performed by the public sector. We will discuss the importance of both factors.

If exports represent a low share of total output, a policy of rapid and drastic opening up of the economy to trade may imply losses in production and employment in the import substitution sectors that will be much higher than any conceivable expansion originating in exports. Even if exports do grow very rapidly, as was the case in Brazil, their relative share in GDP cannot compensate for the output loss elsewhere in the economy.

On the other hand, the reallocation of resources away from import substitution industries and toward the export sector is a slow process. It requires capacity expansions in the export activities. It also requires that the necessary complementary investment in infrastructure be forthcoming. This process takes more time than the fall in output and employment in the import substituting sectors. Thus, an almost unavoidable effect of rapid tariff reduction is to generate a large recession in the economy. If this is accompanied by contractionary fiscal and monetary policies, these negative effects will be reinforced.

What the previous reasoning implies is not that the shift to the new policies would not be possible. Given the relative size of the external sector and provided the government has some preference for less recession and unemployment, what it means is that a better transition path is a slow one. And this was the course followed by Brazil in the 1960s. The opening up to foreign trade through tariff reductions took place in Brazil only in the fourth year of the stabilization policy. During 1967, the tariff reform which, in any case, was quite moderate (see Table 1) was implemented by bringing tariffs down to an average of 41%. In addition, tariff reductions were not uniform. Internal production of durable and nondurable consumer goods continued to enjoy a high degree of protection after the reform. Average nominal tariffs in these sectors were reduced only to 116% and 56%, respectively, at their lowest point (in 1967). What these figures indicate is that Brazilian industry was allowed to adapt gradually to the new conditions without severe repercussions in industrial production.

On the other hand, the development pattern pursued by Brazil, consistent with these tariff reductions, represented an effort to pursue a balanced growth of industry oriented to the domestic sector and toward exports. It consisted in taking advantage of the existing capacity to expand the durable goods sector, construction activities, the capital goods sector—all

TABLE 1
Tariffs: Brazil
(percentages)*

	1966	1967	1969
Nondurable goods	152	56	82
Durable consumer goods	260	116	176
Intermediate goods	76	36	45
Capital goods	60	40	40
Manufacturing sector	114	49	67
Agriculture	83	32	32
Average for the economy	98	41	53

*These are nominal rates plus extra charges (such as deposits required previous to importing) and surtax rates on certain imported products.

Source:

A. Fishlow, "Foreign Trade Regimes and Economic Development: Brazil," *National Bureau of Economic Research* (mimeo), no date.

mainly oriented to the domestic market—and exports. This pattern can be observed in Table 2. What it meant in practice was that the strategy of gradually opening up the economy did not result in large output losses or high unemployment because of the compensating role played by the expansion of industry oriented to the domestic market. A reasonable balance was achieved between stabilization goals, opening up to trade objectives, and high employment. The consequences of its alternative radical counterpart will be observed in the next chapters dealing with the Chilean case.

A second constraint facing policymakers, besides the high importance of domestic vis-à-vis external demand, was the predominant role played by public investment in Brazil. This was recognized, and in fact public investment played a significant countercyclical role. This was another sign of a movement away from rigid orthodoxy in the Brazilian case. The share of

TABLE 2

Industrial Growth and Exports: Brazil
(rates of growth, percentages)

	1965–1967	1967–1970
Durable consumer goods	13.4	21.9
Nondurable consumer goods	3.6	9.7
Capital goods	4.5	13.7
Intermediate goods	10.8	13.7
Exports	5.9	10.7

Source:
M. C. Tavares and L. Belluzzo, "Notas sobre o proceso de industrializacao recente no Brasil," paper presented to the U.N. Economic Commission for Latin America (CEPAL) meeting on industrialization in Latin America, Oct. 1978; in CEPAL, "Políticas de promoción de exportaciones," vol. 5, Santiago, 1978.

public investment in the total had been historically high. It was likely that private investment would go down during the stabilization phase, as in fact it did. Instead of retreating and leaving the investment function to the private sector as the more radical version of orthodoxy in the 1970s would dictate, the public sector stepped in and increased its programs.

In fact, during the first phase of the stabilization program, the government was faced with a difficult option: either it waited for the domestic private sector to gain confidence and invest or the government would take an active role, providing the resources and undertaking the new projects needed to stimulate the economy out of the recession. It is clear from Table 3 that the option taken was the last one. It can be seen that public investment played an important role from the very beginning of the stabilization program. Government investment rose 7.9% and that of state enterprises 70.5% during 1965. This trend was maintained in the following years, with the exception of 1966, when fiscal balance became a high priority goal.

Sources:
For the federal government deficit:
A. Foxley, "Stabilization Policies and Stagflation: The Cases of Brazil and Chile," in A. Foxley and L. Whitehead, eds., *Economic Stabilization in Latin America: Political Dimensions* (Pergamon, 1980); for public investment: estimates of J. R. Wells, quoted in ibid. The estimate includes the federal government, "autarquias," state governments, municipalities, and state enterprises ("autarquias" are decentralized government agencies).

TABLE 3

Fiscal Deficit and Public Investment: Brazil

	Investment (annual growth rate, %)	
Year	Federal, States and munici- palities	State enterprises
1963	−7.9	−17.3
1964	5.2	11.7
1965	7.9	70.5
1966	−4.6	4.9
1967	17.3	22.6
1968	0.6	11.7
1969	16.1	24.9
1970	11.7	25.0

In sum, flexibility and early recognition of structural constraints were features of the post-1964 Brazilian economic policies. These characteristics explain the low doses of orthodoxy in the stabilization package and the relatively mild economic recession that accompanied it. An equivalent stabilization experience in Argentina between 1967 and 1970 during the military government of Onganía shows similar features.

Why the Economic Policies Are More Radical in the 1970s and 1980s

Why was this not so in Chile and Argentina in the 1970s and 1980s? As was suggested before, several factors were present that pushed in the direction of more radical and rigid orthodox policies. These were related to (1) the magnitude of the inherited economic disequilibria, (2) the intensity of the political stalemate and crisis, (3) the degree of threat to existing institutions as perceived by the private sector, which, in turn, was a function of the depth of the transformation of the economy and society in a socialist direction, and (4) the effect of changes in the international economy.

The initial economic conditions in Argentina and Chile in the 1970s were much worse than any comparable situation in the 1960s. Inflation in Argentina was running at monthly rates close to 30% in 1976 whereas a decade earlier, when Onganía took power, that had been the rate of inflation for the whole year. Indeed, things had turned for the worse after the 1960s in Argentina. The Chilean economy was in no better shape during 1973. Yearly inflation was also at the three-digit level, markets were seriously disrupted, generalized scarcity of basic goods coexisted with extended black markets, and production was falling.

It would be naive to explain this drastic economic deterioration in Argentina and Chile as simply a result of wrong economic policies although these certainly played a significant role. Monetary, fiscal, and wage expansion coexisting with controlled prices, negative real interest rates, and fixed exchange rates could not but generate large sectoral imbalances that would be ultimately reflected in rampaging inflation, the breakdown of large parts of the productive system, and a generalized scarcity of essential goods.

In a sense, these inadequate policies reflected, at least in part, a rather desperate attempt to rescue political and economic experiments that had sought to solve the old problems of slower growth, higher inflation, and distributive contradictions from a radical populist and socialist perspective.[6] After a long succession of the most diverse economic-political formu-

6. Kaufman has stressed this point in his excellent comparative study "Industrial Change."

las that had been attempted in Argentina and Chile in the 1950s and 1960s in order to break the economic deadlock and political immobility, the Perón and Allende governments were showing the enormous failure of yet two more experiments.

But this time the economic crisis had been concurrent with a deep crisis in the political system. Political participation was on the rise. The popular sectors had been establishing a powerful claim on resources in the form of increased income shares and enlarged access to public services, housing, and property ownership. They were also pressing for increased access to and influence over political institutions, the media, the universities, and various means of cultural expression.

This "threatening" presence of the masses resulted in a rapidly escalating social conflict that generalized to all levels of political and social activities. The private sector reacted by withdrawing resources for investment. The more radical the schemes pushed by the government, the larger the withdrawal. Since the economy was in disarray and not growing, it was increasingly difficult to meet the needs of redistributing income and increased capital accumulation without resorting to more drastic (and more antagonistic) redistributive policies—like expropriation of assets—or to the easier expedient of more inflation. These processes eventually led to the breakdown of the political and institutional system and gave way to new authoritarian regimes.

The new military governments imposed a rigid and drastic economic program as a reaction to "economic chaos." It constituted a complete reversal of previous policies, and its objective was not only to bring the economy back to equilibrium but also to discipline the economic and social groups until they adhered to a new rationality.

At this point the main task of the policymakers was to make the policy package a credible one. To achieve this, the government had to apply—with no vacillation or concessions—the policy that had been decided upon as the best one to deal with the situation. One must go all the way with the orthodox economic package, irrespective of how the situation evolves or how the policies affect the population. The most clear example of this approach is provided by the Chilean stabilization policies after 1973, as will be illustrated in the next chapters.

What are the most critical problems as perceived by policymakers at this stage? One is the balance of payments deficit and the other is low investment. For both problems to be solved without resorting to active government intervention—something radical orthodoxy will try to avoid—it becomes essential to restore the confidence of the business community and international financial centers. They will provide badly needed capital that will finance the trade deficit and raise investment.

In order to restore the confidence of these groups and make the economic program credible as a long-term solution to the country's problems, the new policies must conform to certain rules. These rules of "sound economic management" are perfectly codified by the international financial community, including the International Monetary Fund (IMF), large private international banks, and business groups. They consist of reducing the rate of expansion in money supply, eliminating the fiscal deficit, devaluing domestic currency, deregulating prices and private sector activities, and opening up the economy to free trade. Given such an explicit codification of what constitutes sound policies, the restoration of confidence requires strictly abiding by them. In doing so, the economic policies acquire a distinct orthodox flavor.

Why do they also become more radical in a political sense? The depth of the transformation of the economy in a noncapitalist direction previous to the crisis forces a new dimension into the orthodox policies. If there was expropriation of assets and land in the previous economic scheme, the new policies will almost certainly seek not only to reverse the trend but to proceed to privatize as many public enterprises and public sector activities as possible. Dismantling the public sector may seem the most effective way to ensure that the socialist "threat" will not be repeated. More generally, it is likely that the deeper the previous transformation, the greater the emphasis will be in the new economic policies on long-term transformation in the opposite direction. In these cases, the orthodox short-term stabilization scheme will be indissolubly married to a radical, long-term conservative project. Again the Chilean case provides the best example of this.[7]

Finally, a political factor is again important in explaining the radical nature of the policies. After the coup, the destruction of most institutions that regulated political participation within the previous democratic framework creates the space necessary for the state to act with a substantial amount of autonomy regarding civil society. This autonomy expresses itself not only with respect to those groups in the opposition but also in relation to large segments of groups sympathetic to the regime, like white-collar workers, independent producers, small farmers, etc. The state need not be responsive to their demands or complaints. It has power. So it has time and "space," given the disarticulation of civil society, to undertake whatever changes are needed in order to infuse a "new rationality" into economic and political behavior. The state is the nation, and those in power (the military, the technocrats, and those few enlightened businessmen) are the depository of the new rationality. They must proceed without compromising to make it work. Once the economic program has been defined, they must stick to it. Recession, unemployment, and bankruptcies are indeed healthy signs that the medicine is being administered after all.[8]

7. See ibid.
8. G. O'Donnell, *Antecedentes para el Estudio del Estado Burocrático-Autoritario* (provisional title), unpubl. ms. O'Donnell's ideas have been very influential on my own concerning topics covered in this section.

In sum, the turn toward radical orthodox policies in the 1970s seems to have been influenced by a number of new factors: an intensification of economic imbalances as a result of objective problems in the industrialization strategy and inadequate economic policies; a deepening of the crisis in the political system, influenced by a larger participation of popular groups in decision making and the threat that this process implied to the business sector; a crisis of confidence in the economic and political formulas that had been attempted and the need to restore the confidence of such key groups as foreign capitalists and domestic business groups by turning toward internationally codified "rational economic policies"; and, given the severity of institutional breakdown that accompanied the regime and policy change, a higher degree of autonomy of the state vis-à-vis civil society that allowed the government to attempt bold and radical experiments within the framework of monetarist ideas.

Changes in the International Economy: Effects on the Nature of Economic Policies in the 1960s and 1970s

We have so far discussed the influence of domestic economic and political factors on stabilization policies. It is now time to refer to changes in the world economy and their effects on policy choice in the 1960s and 1970s.

The world economy in the 1960s passed through a period of sustained growth, expanded trade, and relatively orderly international financial flows. The industrialized countries' economies expanded at an average rate close to 5% per annum, as can be seen in Table 4. The growth of world trade was even more impressive, expanding at a rate of 9% a year between

TABLE 4

Growth Performance in Industrialized Countries
(GDP average annual growth rates, percentages)

	1960–1970	1970–1980
North America	4.0	3.3
Japan and Oceania	9.4	5.1
Western Europe	4.7	2.9
All industrialized countries	4.9	3.4

Source:
World Bank, *World Development Report* (Oxford University Press, 1979).

1965 and 1973. This allowed for a rapid increase of developing countries' exports, which grew at 6.4% a year during the same period.

The unprecedented boom in the international economy made it possible for some developing countries—particularly in Asia and a few in Latin America—to take full advantage of expanded trade, embarking on outward-looking, export-oriented development strategies, which by the early 1970s were often acclaimed as "success stories," showing the way for other developing economies to follow.

Events in the international economy in the 1970s were less favorable. Beginning with the U.S. balance of payments problems and the dollar crisis in 1971 and followed by the upsurge in food and oil prices in 1973–1974 and the subsequent disarray in international finances, the decade was characterized by high world inflation, frequent price shocks, slower growth rates for industrialized countries, higher unemployment, unstable balance of payments for most countries, and more limited trade opportunities. Growth rates in the developed world decreased to an average of 3.4% per year. The volume of world trade increased 4% a year, less than one-half of what had been achieved in the previous decade. The exports of less developed countries (LDC) grew only 3.6% a year after the oil crisis as compared with 6.4% in the previous eight-year period.

These negative trends were the natural consequence of world recession, exchange rate and balance of payments instability, and increased protectionist measures undertaken by the industrialized countries. The protectionist trend expanded from sectors such as clothing and textiles to footwear and steel. The effect on developing countries' exports was almost immediate. The World Bank has estimated that, as a result of this policy, the exports of LDCs in these four sectors decreased in volume as early as 1977.[9]

Perhaps even more important from the point of view of our topic, the world economy was subject in the 1970s to periodic and unexpected external shocks originating mainly, but not exclusively, in the unstable prices of some key commodities. Given this new, highly volatile international environment, the national economies had to adjust to a whole new set of parameters, including much higher international inflationary pressures and stagflationary trends both at home and abroad.

How did these international events affect the course of domestic economic policies, particularly stabilization, in the context of the Latin American economies? During the 1960s, the relative importance of external inflation, as compared with internal inflationary pressures, was much lower than in the 1970s. The sources of inflation were quite predictable: either excess demand due to expansionary government policies and high propensities to consume or cost-push factors originating mainly in the administered-price sector of the economy. It was accepted that these pressures could be reinforced by inflationary expectations. But, on the whole, the debate centered on which of these two sets of factors was the predominant

9. World Bank, *World Development Report* (Oxford University Press, 1979).

cause behind the price increases. Fiscal-monetary discipline was one course of action. Acting directly over costs and expectations was an alternative policy course. But in practice the stabilization effort, while emphasizing one or the other, usually ended up producing a mixed policy package, with ingredients from both. In the 1970s, the international component in domestic inflation was much larger. It was going to significantly alter the normal functioning of the domestic economy. The search for adequate policies to deal with this new phenomenon would not exclude the more radical versions of monetarist-conservative doctrines.

As has been previously suggested, another factor influencing policy choice was the rate of expansion in world trade, which was very significant in the 1960s. Countries soon recognized that significant advantages could be gained from international trade so that cautiously, given inherited import substitution biases, the countries moved in the direction of fewer trade restrictions. This was the case in both Argentina in 1967 and Brazil in 1964. But, more important, export promotion was to become a key feature of the stabilization program. Export expansion would help in checking recessionary tendencies induced by the stabilization policies. It would also make higher growth rates possible after the recession was over.

During the 1970s the situation was rapidly changing. Policymakers were subject to two different and, on the surface, opposite forces. One originated in the appeal of successful trade-oriented development stories of the 1960s. Some newly industrialized countries in Asia and Latin America had been able to grow rapidly and to keep inflation under control by pursuing outward and market-oriented economic policies. The inclination to pursue the same course and thus repeat the "success stories" during the 1970s was almost irresistible.

But a countervailing force resulted, generated not by ideology or past experience but by new facts and signals emanating from the international economy. Suddenly, the same countries in the north that had been pressing for lower tariffs were limiting the access of Latin American exports to their domestic markets. The industrialized economies were facing recession and large unemployment. On the other hand, there was no predictable course for international prices. The cost of raw materials was subject to wide fluctuations and supply disruptions. And, above all, international inflation rates had gone up sharply, making stability conditions in the domestic economy all the more difficult to obtain.

These factors pushed in the direction of more cautious policies, at least insofar as the external sector and the opening up to trade strategies were concerned. After all, a relatively obvious response to increased inflationary shocks from abroad was not to expose the economy domestically to the full impact of the multiple external shocks. And, indeed, some countries like Brazil and Colombia attempted to pursue such a course.

Other countries did not react in this manner. Latin America, faced with three-digit inflation in the early 1970s, attempted simultaneously to eliminate inflation through orthodox instruments and to open up the economy to free trade and free capital movements. Why was this risky path followed? A part of the answer has just been suggested. The excitement with the successful stories of the 1960s had not faded. The emergence of right-wing authoritarian regimes, in all the Southern Cone countries, created the unique political opportunity to emulate those experiences, something that had not been possible previously given conflicting group interests and ideologies.

Another factor influencing the choice of uncompromising radical stabilization policies was the deterioration in trade suffered by some countries in the 1970s. For example, although Brazil had not experienced marked fluctuations in trade during the 1960s, Chile faced a significant deterioration particularly in 1975 as a result of the oil crisis. This deterioration led to a loss of income compared with the rest of the world equivalent to 5.6% of the GDP in Chile in 1975. An external shock of this magnitude had the effect of rapidly persuading economic policymakers and the military of the advantages of a drastic contractionary shock that would allow the economy to reduce the demand for imports, thus overcoming balance of payments difficulties. This was the beginning, in early 1975, of the strict orthodox policies that were to persist in Chile long after the external crisis was over.

The impact of the crisis in the developed countries had an additional indirect effect in policy choice in Latin America. The very severe disarray in the international economy had resulted, as mentioned above, in a rapid worsening of the economic situation in most industrialized countries. Policymakers, using the conventional economic tools, had not been able to solve the stagflation or unemployment problem. A possible explanation would be that this was due to the new nature of inflation in the 1970s and that, consequently, new ways had to be found and new types of policies devised in order to deal with the problem effectively.

An alternative explanation—and one that became rapidly popular with the military and the right-wing coalitions supporting them in Latin America—was that the policies failed because they were not drastic enough. If fiscal discipline, monetary contraction, and free trade were applied consistently for a sufficiently long period of time, inflation and recession would be curbed. The crisis in the national economies was as much a result of changes in the world economy as it was of a secular mismanagement of domestic economic policies. In this sense, the crisis in the international economy had been the detonator of accumulated inefficiencies and misconceived policies. The policy failures originated not only in inadequate prescriptions in the technical sense. They also had to do with not being tough enough in disciplining workers and producers alike through market-oriented, financially sound deflationary policies.

When external shocks and domestic mismanagement worsened the situation to its limit, conditions were ripe to deal with the crisis not through mild, gradualist approaches but rather through a drastic reversal of previous trends and policies.

3

A Radical
Conservative Experiment
Chile After 1973

THE previous chapter dealt with the evolution of orthodox economic stabilization programs in Latin America since the 1960s. It is clear from our discussion that the ideas about stabilization and the specific policies pursued changed significantly during this period. One of the most remarkable changes was the increasingly radical approach to economic stabilization that has gained ground since the 1970s.

Radicalism refers to two main aspects of the new policies. The first one is the predisposition to apply tough "shock treatment" policies when other more gradual approaches have failed. Shock is administered even when its consequences are a long, deep recession, high rates of unemployment, and deterioration in the distribution of income. These negative results can be sustained because of the political context in which the policies are applied.

Radicalism refers also to the stronger component of structural and institutional change in the stabilization policies of the 1970s and 1980s. The idea is that if all other formulas to stabilize the economy have failed, there must be something very wrong with the essential functioning of the economic system and of the political system as well. Until this is corrected, long-term price stability and equilibrium in the balance of payments will not be possible. As argued before, this kind of reasoning has a strong structuralist flavor.

Proposed structural changes have a distinct free market orientation. The main elements are (1) a policy of privatization of economic activities accompanied by a withdrawal of the state from its regulatory and developmental functions, (2) an opening up of the economy to international trade and financial flows, and (3) free market policies as regards price determination and capital markets. Institutional changes refer to modifications in labor legislation, social security reform, the development of new private schemes for the provision of social services, and regional decentralization. In the political sphere, institutional changes may include, as in Chile, drafting a new constitution that drastically modifies the main political institutions and decision-making processes.

The economic policies in Argentina after 1976 and in Chile and Uruguay after 1973 share this emphasis on long-run structural and institutional changes although they differ in the timing and the intensity of the proposed changes. Of the three, Chile is the country where these neoconservative policies and reforms have been applied in a more radical and consistent fashion. In this sense it gets close to being a test of "the pure case."

It is for this reason that we will concentrate in this chapter and the next on a detailed evaluation of the Chilean case. We hope that some important lessons can be learned by looking in depth at Chile's economic policies and institutional reforms after 1973. Our analysis here will center on three aspects: macroeconomic policies and performance, a detailed discussion of short-term stabilization policies and the various phases that can be identified in the stabilization program, and the impact of structural changes in the Chilean economy.

In the next chapter we will deal with revolutionary changes in existing institutions. A thorough understanding of the meaning of these reforms requires a knowledge of the underlying ideology in the radical conservative project. We will discuss both these topics in the next chapter whereas in the present chapter we will concentrate on economic policies and structural changes in the sphere of the economy.

Results of the Stabilization Program

Just as occurred in the Brazilian case, the economic policy of Chile in the period after 1973 has been the object of a profound controversy. The economic results for this period are interpreted as a resounding success by some and as quite negative by others. As we will see, two different economic stories can be constructed, depending on the indicators that are selected to evaluate the economy's performance.

Indicators which usually are cited as the basis for arguing the success of Chile's economic policy are presented in Table 5. These indicators show by column: (1) a reduction in the annual rate of inflation from 369.2% in 1974 to 31.2% in 1980;[1] (2) the achievement of high rates of growth for the GDP from 1977 to 1980 following the deep recession provoked by the "shock treatment" administered in 1975; (3) a significant reduction in the fiscal deficit so that it was eliminated in 1979; (4) the dynamic growth of nontraditional exports, which tripled between 1974 and 1980; (5) an accelerating net inflow of foreign capital that reached more than $1,600 million per year in the period 1978–1980 and was the main factor behind the accumulation of reserves; (6) a surplus in the balance of payments in the period 1978–1980 as a result of the accumulation of international reserves; and (7) an increase in gross reserves. According to performance standards usually considered by in-

---

1. This corresponds to a twelve-month inflation rate as measured by the Economics Department of the University of Chile.

TABLE 5

Macroeconomic Indicators: Chile

Year	GDP (1)	(1a)	Consumer Prices (2)	Fiscal Deficit (3)	Non-traditional Exports (4)	Net Capital Inflows (5)	Balance of Payments (6)	Gross Reserves (7)
1970	3.5		36.1	2.9	225.9	531.3	226.1	1.006
1974	4.2		369.2	8.0	273.2	275.0	−54.4	645
1975	−16.6	−12.9	343.3	2.9	401.9	323.6	−297.5	463
1976	5.0	3.5	197.9	2.0	510.3	252.4	490.8	880
1977	8.6	9.9	84.2	1.5	588.5	444.0	−7.0	871
1978	6.0	8.2	37.2	0.8	644.9	1.651.8	572.2	1.181
1979	7.2	8.3	38.9	−1.7	874.5	1.697.8	804.4	2.413
1980	6.5		31.2	n.a.	967.1	1.614.7	534.8	2.892

Sources:

(1) ODEPLAN, *Cuentas Nacionales de Chile.* Annual rates of variation are at constant prices. The figures for 1979 correspond to provisional estimates for GDP; see *Informe Gemines*, No. 21, 1979. New National Accounts estimates —column (1 a)—have been given by ODEPLAN in 1981. Unfortunately, the series begins in 1974 which does not allow us to compare economic performance with previous periods. Figures are percentages.

(2) Consumer Price Index from R. Cortázar and J. Marshall, "El índice de precios al consumidor," *Colección Estudios CIEPLAN*, No. 4, 1980. Figures are in millions of dollars.

(3) Treasury Department, *Exposición sobre el Estado de la Hacienda Pública*, Jan. 1978; and ODEPLAN, *Cuentas Nacionales de Chile.* Figures are percentages of GDP.

(4) Central Bank of Chile, in R. Ffrench-Davis, "Políticas de comercio exterior en Chile 1973–1978," CIEPLAN (mimeo), Santiago, 1979. Figures are in millions of dollars in 1977.

(5) Ibid.
(6) Ibid.   (7) Ibid.

ternational credit organizations, particularly the IMF, these results indicate success. They also neatly fit the criteria of private international banks.[2]

A different story can be told by selecting other indicators, such as those which appear in Table 6. These are the kind of variables generally used to argue that the Chilean economic policy has been far from successful. In summarized form, the critical argument contends (by column) that (1) the Chilean economy has grown in the period after 1973 at an average rate that is significantly below the recent historical rate (as can be seen also in per capita terms—(4) in Table 6—this rate has not reached 1 percent per year); (2) economic growth has been even slower in goods-producing sectors; (3) the modest growth that is seen at the aggregate level has been largely due to the expansion of services; (5) the potential for future growth is limited by low rates of gross investment, which have scarcely surpassed 11%; and (6) the employment level has grown slowly in this period, (7) during which there has also been a high rate of unemployment.

These figures are averages for the period. They do not reflect the annual trend of the indicators, particularly for the last years of the period. In fact, the averages, which cover a period characterized by a deep recession that lasted until the middle of 1976, conceal a trend toward recuperation beginning in 1977, which, for some indicators such as GDP, is significant.

A more precise image of these trends can be seen in Table 7, which includes figures that fill in the picture presented by the positive and negative indicators shown in Tables 5 and 6. It is apparent in Table 7 that the trend toward recovery of GDP just reached in 1978 the per capita level of 1970, and only in 1979 surpassed the per capita level of 1974. Table 7 also shows a

2. I. Friedman, "The Role of Private Banks in Stabilization Programs," in W. Cline and S. Weintraub, eds., *Economic Stabilization in Developing Countries* (Brookings Institution, 1981).

slow recovery of the rate of investment beginning in 1977— column (4). This slow recovery suggests that the possibility of maintaining the high rate of growth of GDP observed in the 1977–1980 period should be viewed cautiously. On the other hand, the surplus in the balance of payments observed in Table 5 was accompanied by a marked trend toward a deficit in the current account (and also in the trade balance), which was

TABLE 6

Other Macro Results: Chile*

(percentages)

		1960–1970	1974–1980
(1)	GDP	4.5	3.3
(2)	Production of goods	4.5	1.9
(3)	Production of services	4.4	4.5
(4)	GDP per capita	2.3	1.5
(5)	Rate of investment	15.3	11.1
(6)	Total employment	2.1	0.9
(7)	Rate of unemployment	6.5	13.3

*We were forced to use the old estimates of National Accounts by ODEPLAN as the only way of having comparable figures for 1960–1970 and 1974–1980. New revised estimates begin in 1974.

Sources:

(1) ODEPLAN, old National Accounts and estimates from *Informe Gemines,* No. 21, 1979, annual variation rates.

(2) Ibid.; the production of goods includes agriculture, fishing, mining, industry, and construction.

(3) Ibid.; the production of services includes electricity, gas and water, transportation, trade, and other services.

(4) Ibid.

(5) Ibid.; and *Comentarios sobre la situación económica,* Department of Economics, University of Chile, 1st semester, 1979. Investment in fixed capital over GDP.

(6) R. Cortázar, "Desempleo, Polreza, y Distribución, Chile 1970–1981," *Apuntes CIEPLAN,* No. 34, 1982. Employment figures exclude Minimum Employment Program (PEM).

(7) Ibid.

TABLE 7
Economic and Social Indicators: Chile

	1970	1974	1975	1976	1977	1978	1979	1980
(1) GDP per Capita	100.0	102.4	89.3	91.4	97.6	101.7	107.4	111.6
(2) Balance in Current Account	−159.9	−254.3	−532.3	143.5	−531.0	−952.8	−911.8	−1.100.6
(3) Debt Service Ratio Over	33.5	18.6	40.0	44.2	49.2	46.4	42.3	38.7
(4) Investment Rate	15.0	13.0	10.7	9.8	10.6	11.3	12.0	14.0
(5) Total Employment	100.0	104.6	99.0	94.9	99.3	102.7	103.5	109.3
(6) Employed in Pop. of 12 Years and Over	42.9	40.4	37.4	35.0	35.8	36.2	36.3	
(7) Unemployment Rate: Without PEM	6.1	9.2	13.4	16.3	14.0	13.9	13.8	10.6
(8) With PEM	6.1	9.2	15.5	21.8	19.8	18.4	17.8	15.9
(9) Real Salaries and Wages	100.0	65.1	62.9	64.8	71.5	76.0	82.3	89.2
(10) Salaries and Wages as Share of National Income	44.3	34.6	34.7	34.7	—	—	—	
(11) Consumption of the: Poorer 20%	7.6					5.2	—	—
Richer 20%	44.5					51.0	—	—
(12) Average Pension	100.0	59.3	52.0	56.4	60.9	67.0	75.9	n.a.

(13) Housing Construction, Avg. per Person	100.0	85.3	49.8	38.4	42.0	44.2	—	n.a.
(14) Enrollment in Pop. of 10–20 Years of Age	100.0	113.1	—	—	116.3	115.2	—	n.a.
(15) Enrollment in 1st Grade in Corresponding Pop.	100.0	106.3	99.4	94.3	96.2	—	—	n.a.
(16) Hospital Beds per Person	100.0	94.4	91.7	88.9	86.1	83.3	—	n.a.
(17) Health Service per Person	100.0	89.3	84.5	90.3	91.3	94.2	—	n.a.

Sources:

(1) Old estimates of National Accounts by ODEPLAN, *Informe Gemines*, No. 21, 1979, annual variation rates. Figures for 1979 and 1980 are estimates from *Comentarios sobre la situación económica*, Department of Economics, University of Chile, 2nd semester, 1980.

(2) Central Bank of Chile, in R. Ffrench-Davis, "Políticas de comercio exterior en Chile 1973–1978," CIEPLAN (mimeo), Santiago, 1979. Figures are in millions of dollars in 1977.

(3) Central Bank of Chile.

(4) ODEPLAN, *Informe Gemines*, No. 21, 1979; and *Comentarios*.

(5) P. Meller, R. Cortázar, and J. Marshall, "La evolución del empleo en Chile 1974–1978," *Colección Estudios CIEPLAN*, No. 3, Santiago, 1979.

(6) Ibid.

(7) Ibid.

(8) Unemployment rate including Minimum Employment Program (PEM), ibid.

(9) *Comentarios*.

(10) ODEPLAN, *Informe Gemines*, No. 21, 1979.

(11) INE, *Encuesta de Presupuestos Familiares*, 1969 and 1978.

(12) Superintendency of Social Service.

(13) ODEPLAN, *Informe Gemines*, No. 21, 1979; and estimates for 1977 and 1979 based on *Comentarios*.

(14) INE, *Compendio Estadístico*.

(15) E. Schiefelbein and M. Grossi, *Análisis de la matrícula escolar en Chile*, CIDE, 1978.

(16) INE, *Compendio Estadístico*.

(17) Ibid.

compensated by with an influx of loans from abroad. The debt service ratio rose over 40% of exports in 1975 and stayed there until 1980.

One of the most striking aspects of the Chilean economic experience from 1973 to 1980 was the simultaneous deterioration of employment, wages, per capita consumption, and other social indicators that measure the population's access to housing, education, and health, as well as the skewing of consumption by income strata. These figures are also shown in Table 7.

The trend toward recovery reflected in the social welfare indicators was not very significant. The national unemployment rate remained above 13%. When the so-called Minimum Employment Program (PEM) is included in the unemployment figure, rates go up to 18% in 1979 and 17% in 1980. PEM is a make-work employment program where the unemployed are hired and paid around $30 a month, equivalent to one-fourth the legal wage. Real wages and salaries in 1980 were still 10% below the 1970 level.

In brief, economic results for Chile in the 1973–1980 period give mixed signs: the rate of inflation decreased, after a deep recession GDP reached prerecession levels; the fiscal deficit was eliminated; there was an accumulation of reserves, and nontraditional exports expanded rapidly. At the same time, a low investment rate, a significant deficit in the commercial balance, increasing external indebtedness, high unemployment, real wage reduction, and a deterioration in the distribution of income, consumption, and basic social services were among the negative factors.

In order to get a better understanding of how these results were achieved, we will discuss in more detail in the next section the stabilization policies and the various phases that can be distinguished in the period 1973–1980, signaling changes in policies or in the objectives of the stabilization program.

The Stabilization Program
and Its Phases

The stabilization program in Chile can be separated into four different phases.[3] The first one we will call "deregulation"; the second consists of the so-called "shock treatment"; the third one centers in curbing expectations; and the fourth phase corresponds to the global monetarist approach. The main economic indicators for all four phases are given in Table 8 where trends for the various phases can be easily identified.

Phase 1: Deregulation,
September 1973 –March 1975

The main objective of phase 1 was to restitute market mechanisms in an economy with extended controls and severe imbalances. Setting prices right was the first task, and this was done by devaluing domestic currency and by freeing up prices, except for thirty products whose prices were deregulated more gradually. The exchange rate was devalued by 230% between September and October 1973. A second objective of the policy was to reduce the public sector deficit by decreasing government expenditures and increasing taxes. The main tax changes consisted of the introduction of a 20% value-added tax while at the same time several direct taxes affecting capital were reduced or eliminated: the tax on corporate profits was reduced and the net wealth and capital gains taxes were

3. For a good description of the policies and their interrelationship with social behavior and ideology, see T. Moulian and P. Vergara, "Estado, ideología y políticas económicas en Chile 1973–1978," *Colección Estudios CIEPLAN,* No. 3, 1980; and T. Moulian and P. Vergara, "Políticas de estabilización y comportamientos sociales: La experiencia chilena 1973–1978," *Apuntes CIE-PLAN,* No. 22, 1980.

TABLE 8   Phases in the Stabilization Program, Chile 1973–1979

		CPI (1)†	BP (2)	IIP (3)	UNEM (4)	PCU (5)	ER (6)	TAR (7)	ERM (8)	M_1 (9)	M_2 (10)	inon (11)	i_r^Y (12)	w* (13)
							Phase 1							
1973	II	51.9		106.3	3.1	73.9				32.1	31.8			
	III	64.3		101.2	—	91.4	9.2			49.3	49.2			
	IV	128.5		122.5	7.0	99.3	30.1	94.0	58.4	45.4	45.7			
1974	I	45.3	59.5	109.8	9.2	106.9	29.6	92.3	56.9	63.2	64.2			63.4
	II	46.6	180.3	113.8	10.3	126.3	32.9	76.3	58.0	30.9	29.9			64.5
	III	46.8	-3.9	111.0	9.4	78.4	33.3	67.0	55.6	28.1	27.8			63.7
	IV	44.7	-375.6	109.7	9.7	62.0	37.1	67.0	62.0	28.1	30.8	9.6	-24.4	68.5
1975	I	46.5	-189.3	93.1	13.3	57.8	45.0	54.7	69.6	44.8	51.9	9.6	-49.3	64.9
							Phase 2							
1975	I	46.5	-189.3	93.1	13.3	57.8	45.0	54.7	69.6	44.8	51.9	9.6	-49.3	64.9
	II	67.8	-82.5	88.8	16.1	57.1	46.7	52.0	71.0	25.0	38.7	16.5	-23.4	60.4
	III	41.4	44.1	73.5	16.6	56.1	45.2	47.7	66.8	45.0	57.2	19.7	178.4	63.2
	IV	29.4	-47.0	85.2	18.7	53.1	44.9	44.0	64.7	38.2	35.1	12.8	65.7	63.1
1976	I	36.4	136.6	90.4	19.8	56.6	44.3	40.7	62.3	37.2	39.8	14.6	18.2	62.1
	II	38.8	94.4	93.5	18.0	69.2	40.5	36.7	55.4	22.8	38.9	14.7	56.4	63.0
							Phase 3							
1976	II	38.8	94.4	93.5	18.0	69.2	40.5	36.7	55.4	22.8	38.9	14.7	56.4	63.0
	III	33.1	134.1	97.1	15.7	70.3	33.6	33.0	44.7	34.7	48.3	11.8	40.9	65.1
	IV	20.0	103.7	100.3	13.6	58.2	34.2	32.3	45.2	26.8	29.1	12.5	101.2	68.8

Year	Qtr													
1977	I	21.4	48.6	98.1	13.9	65.5	32.7	24.3	40.6	45.1	58.3	11.3	52.9	71.7
	II	20.8	7.7	105.4	13.0	62.2	29.0	23.2	35.7	22.9	28.7	7.8	34.5	69.3
	III	13.5	−59.3	107.9	12.8	54.5	29.5	21.6	35.8	14.4	16.6	6.3	23.9	73.7
	IV	12.7	−3.6	104.9	13.2	56.5	31.7	18.5	37.6	11.8	13.7	7.3	45.9	71.1
1978	I	8.7	270.5	103.9	14.7	56.4	33.1	15.3	38.2	30.2	32.2	5.9	47.6	74.8
	II	9.4	129.7	117.1	12.8	59.3	34.5	14.1	39.4	17.1	18.3	5.0	28.3	75.1
	III	9.8	107.6	119.7	13.7	63.6	34.3	13.2	38.8	6.6	15.9	4.7	14.0	76.9
	IV	6.6	109.5	117.5	14.8	68.2	34.5	12.2	38.7	9.8	21.1	5.5	52.9	77.1
1979	I	6.6	339.9	122.1	16.5	85.5	33.8	11.4	37.7	21.7	24.2	4.4	29.8	81.0
	II	7.7	211.8	123.2	12.5	92.6	34.1	10.5	37.7	9.9	9.0	4.0	19.6	82.2
							Phase 4							
1979	II	7.7	211.8	123.2	12.5	92.6	34.1	10.5	37.7	9.9	9.0	4.0	19.6	82.2
	III	11.0	289.4	126.0	12.5	89.0	33.7	10.2	37.1	7.2	13.3	4.0	−1.2	83.2
	IV	9.0	206.8	125.2	12.7	96.4	31.8	10.2	35.0	11.3	11.2	4.0	23.9	82.8
1980	I	6.7	411.9	126.2	12.8	118.4	30.5	10.2	33.6	16.6	13.9	4.1	23.9	86.7
	II	7.5	150.3	128.0	11.7	92.7	28.9	10.2	31.8	13.9	9.8	3.1	10.0	89.1
	III	6.4	228.5	131.5	11.8	95.5	23.8	10.2	30.6	7.2	12.5	2.9	9.9	88.4
	IV	7.7	−15.3	130.8	10.7	89.7	26.2	10.2	28.8	13.7	14.3	3.0	6.2	92.6
1981	I	4.3	−192.3	129.7	11.3	83.0	25.3*	10.2	27.8*	12.4*	19.2*	3.6	37.7	92.9
	II	2.8	−207.7	132.9	9.0	79.6	24.0*	10.2	26.4*	13.1*	14.6*	3.5	36.1	94.5
	III	2.3	−3.9	134.4	10.5	78.3	23.5*	10.2	25.9*	−4.2*	13.3*	3.5	36.1	99.8
	IV	1.6	−181.9	120.2	13.5	75.2		10.2		5.4*	3.9*	3.7	49.4	102.2

*Index of wages and salaries with base 1970=100.
†Sources on following page.

eliminated. Additional contraction in demand was pursued by attempting to reduce the rate of expansion in money supply and by a contraction in real wages.

Other objectives consisted of preparing the ground for long-term structural changes. Policy measures in this area were varied. They consisted of returning to previous owners private property that had been taken over by workers or by the government. Previously expropriated American companies, mainly in the copper sectors, were compensated for by a presumed underpayment. New norms liberalizing imports and requirements for foreign investment, proposing across-the-board tariff reductions, setting the rules for a privatization of public enterprises, and stimulating the development of a private

---

Sources (Table 8):

(1)   CPI: Consumer Price Index from R. Cortázar and J. Marshall, "El índice de precios al consumidor," *Colección Estudios CIEPLAN*, No. 4, 1980.

(2)   BP: Net accumulation of reserves balance of payments; Central Bank of Chile.

(3)   IIP: Index of Industrial Production seasonally adjusted; SOFOFA.

(4) UNEM: Rate of unemployment for Greater Santiago; Economics Department, University of Chile.

(5)   PCU: Price of copper, U.S. cents per pound; Central Bank of Chile.

(6)   ER: Real exchange rate, pesos per dollar, in Dec. 1978 prices; Central Bank of Chile.

(7)   TAR: Average nominal tariffs; Central Bank of Chile.

(8)   ERM: Reach exchange rate for imports (real exchange rate corrected for changes in tariffs); R. Ffrench-Davis, "Políticas de comercio exterior en Chile 1973–1978," CIEPLAN (mimeo), Santiago, 1979.

(9) M_1: Rate of growth nominal money supply, defined as currency plus demand deposits; Central Bank of Chile.

(10) M_2: Rate of growth nominal money supply, defined as currency plus demand and time deposits; Central Bank of Chile.

(11) i_{non}: Thirty-day nominal interest rate; Central Bank of Chile.

(12) i_r^Y: Yearly equivalent of thirty-day *real* interest rate; Central Bank of Chile and CPI by Cortázar and Marshall, CPI "El índice."

(13)   w: Real wages and salaries index based on CPI and official figures for nominal wages and salaries; INE.

capital market were enforced. Collective bargaining was suppressed, and labor union activities were severely curtailed.

The course followed by the main macrovariables are shown in Table 8. The abrupt deregulation of prices led to a rate of inflation of 128.5% in the last quarter of 1973 (87.6% in October alone where the average monthly rate between January and September had been 14.6%). But the dramatic upsurge in prices, reflecting previous repressed inflation and a price overshoot after deregulation, was not followed by similarly high rates in the next months. In fact, the price increases stabilized around 45% per quarter—column (1)—(14% a month) during this phase, an average rate similar to that prevailing in the last year of the Allende government.

As a result of free prices, firms were stimulated into replenishing their low level of stocks, a result of strict price controls and high inflation throughout 1972 and 1973. Industrial production expanded in the last quarter of 1973, but stabilized at a lower level during 1974, as is readily observed in column (3). In early 1975, clear recessionary signs were present: industrial production in the first quarter was 15% below that of the last quarter of 1974. The recession was the consequence of a drastic reduction in real cash balances in the last quarter of 1973, as can be seen in Table 8 when comparing the expansion of nominal money supply and that of prices. The increase in prices almost tripled the increase in the quantity of money. Monetary contraction was reinforced by a fall in real wages, which reached around 40%, column (13), when compared with 1970 levels.

The unemployment rate was rapidly responsive to the new policies: during the first three months it doubled, reaching 7% in the last quarter of 1973. It was to stay around 9.5% throughout 1974 and jump to 13.3% in the first quarter of 1975, column (4).

The recession was not more severe during 1974 mainly due to an expansionary fiscal policy in spite of stated objectives to the contrary. Public investment increased, particularly in the first quarter. It was hoped, at this stage, that a reduction in public subsidies and employment would bring the fiscal accounts in balance without having to resort to reductions in public investment. A new finance minister in July 1974 did not share this view and attempted to reverse the expansionary trend by curtailing budget expenditures by 15% and public employment by 50,000 persons. At the same time, subsidies to public enterprises were ended. It was this contractionary fiscal policy, sustained while the rate of inflation was accelerating and other components of aggregate demand were falling, that generated the more severe recession of early 1975.

One of the main concerns during this phase was the balance of payments aggravated by the problems encountered by the government in rescheduling the external debt. The policies designed to reduce the external sector deficit paid off in a rather brief period of time. During the first quarter of 1974, there was already a net accumulation of reserves, a result of rapid export expansion aided by unusually high prices for the main Chilean export, copper, and by the large devaluation of late 1973, column (2).

Exchange rate policy during this period followed the fluctuations in the price of copper. The policy consisted of nonannounced minidevaluations several times per month. When the price of copper was high, as in the first semester of 1974, the exchange rate tended to lag behind domestic inflation. Real devaluations took place when copper prices fell, as was the case in the last two quarters of 1974, column (6).

Tariff reductions were announced at the beginning of 1974. They were to take place in a period of three years with a maximum target of 60% for nominal tariffs. This maximum target was reduced to 35% in 1975, with a minimum of 10%. It was expected that the target would be achieved by 1978. The program was implemented gradually during 1974 and early 1975, column (7).

Changes in the financial market allowed for the establishment of private financial companies that operated with no more restrictions than a maximum monthly rate of interest of 25%. The interest rate for banks (which at the time were part of the public sector) was controlled and fixed at 9.6% per month. This discrimination in favor of private financial companies was deliberate in order to stimulate a transfer of funds away from the government and toward the private sector.

By the end of 1974, the rate of inflation had stabilized around 45% per quarter, production figures were showing a decline, and the price of copper fell sharply, which was reflected in a loss of reserves of $375 million in the last quarter alone. The devaluations (30% in December 1974 and an additional 40% in March 1975) were responsible for an increase in the rate of inflation from 9% in December 1974 to 21.4% in April 1975. This bleak picture of recession, accelerated inflation, and balance of payments crisis led to a change in policies. Phase 1 was over. A shock treatment was in order if the negative trends were to be reversed.

Phase 2: The Shock Treatment,
April 1975–June 1976

The new policies consisted of a contractionary shock on demand and a deepening of structural reforms. The demand shock was administered through various channels. Government expenditures were to decrease by 15% in real terms in the domestic component and 25% in the import component during the year. In fact, total expenditures fell by 27% in real terms in 1975, with public investment reduced in half. Tax revenues were to increase by imposing a surcharge on the income tax and eliminating exemptions in the value-added tax. Public enterprises rates were also sharply increased. Real wages were additionally reduced—as can be seen in column (13)—by changing the benchmark against which compensation for cost of living increases was calculated. A make-work employment program was created (the Minimum Employment Program), and a subsidy for firms hiring new workers was established in order to compensate for the negative effects of the recession.

The deepening of long-term structural changes was pursued by three simultaneous channels: more privatization of public enterprises, including the banks that were auctioned at the beginning of this phase; additional stimulus to the development of a private capital market by freeing interest rates charged by banks (once they had been transferred to private hands); and an acceleration in the speed and a lowering of the levels programed for reductions in external tariffs.

A study of the evolution of the main indicators shows mixed results. The rate of increase in the price level diminished from 68% during the second quarter of 1975 to 29% in the last quarter. At the same time, the loss of reserves was curbed during the second quarter, a consequence of a dramatic fall in imports and a continued expansion in nontraditional exports that at least partially compensated for the big loss in copper export revenues. By the end of 1975, the balance of payments was still in deficit, but the trend was encouraging in that the deficit during the second semester had reached only $5 million (compare figures for third and fourth quarters in column [2], Table 8). The situation continued improving in 1976 because the demand for imports was depressed by the recession and exports were still growing fast while the price of copper was slowly recuperating and inflows of short-term capital from abroad increased. The balance of payments showed a surplus of almost $500 million by the end of 1976, as was seen in Table 5.

On the negative side, the policies generated a huge recession. Industrial production fell by 35% in the third quarter of 1975 compared with the same period in 1974. Open unemployment went up to 19.8% in early 1976, column (4), in spite of public make-work employment programs that were fully effective at this time.

The exchange rate policy in this phase was discontinuous. After large real devaluations at the beginning of 1975, the exchange rate remained fairly constant except at the end of the period where it lagged behind domestic inflation, perhaps due to the trend to higher inflation rates in the first two quarters of 1976 (36.4% and 38.8%) as compared with the last quarter of 1975 (29.4%). A constant value for the exchange rate was accompanied by a continued tendency to lower tariffs, columns (6) and (7). As a result, the cost of imports was slowly reduced.

Financial policy and monetary policy offer interesting results. Financial deregulation led to an increase in real interest rates from −23.4% in the second quarter of 1975 to 178.4% in the third quarter, column (12). This abrupt increase generated a cost shock to firms that accentuated stagflationary effects originating in other policy measures, such as demand contraction and devaluation. Monetary policy, on the other hand, was complicated by the drastic reduction in the demand for imports that resulted in accumulation of reserves in the private sector, with an expansionary effect on the monetary base. This is the reason that the monetary shock was really sustained only during the second quarter of 1975.

Unhappiness with a recession that was deeper and longer than expected and the upsurge in inflation during the first quarter of 1976 led to a new change in policies. The strategy to contain inflation was modified, and it was expected that, as a result, inflation would fall and the economy would begin to recuperate in the level of economic activity. Phase 3 was inaugurated with the announcement in June 1976 of a "Program of Economic Recuperation."

Phase 3: Curbing Cost-Push Factors
and Expectations, June 1976–June 1979

The anti-inflation strategy in phase 3 changed in emphasis from demand contraction to curbing cost pressures and expectations. In June 1976 the peso was revalued 10% and a thirty-day preannounced value for future exchange rates was established as a way of reducing costs and influencing inflationary expectations. The exchange rate was revalued again in March 1977. In February 1978 this policy was extended: the value of the exchange rate was announced for the next eleven months. This new approach was complemented by more drastic tariff reductions. Between December 1976 and December 1977 the maximum desired tariff went gradually down until an across-the-board maximum tariff of 10% was established as a target to be achieved in 1979, automobiles being the only exception. The movement toward free trade was reinforced by the withdrawal of the country from the Andean Pact and by a gradual but systematic deregulation of external capital flows that began in October 1977 and was completed in 1979.

Revaluation of domestic currency had a rapid impact on costs, expectations, and the rate of inflation, which decreased to 4.9% a month in August 1976 only to increase again to a monthly rate of 7–8% in the following months. However, the medium-term trend was clear: quarterly rates decreased from around 40% for the second quarter of 1976 to about 13% in the third and fourth quarters of 1977 (accumulated rate for a three-month period). The downward trend continued in 1978, as can be seen in column (1). The quarterly rate of inflation stabilized between 7% and 9% until the end of phase 3 in June 1979.

The reduction in the rate of inflation encouraged an expansion in real wages since nominal wages were indexed to previous inflation. Real wages increased by 5% in the second quarter of 1976 compared with the first quarter, column (13). This was a factor that helped industrial production, which showed an upward trend all through this phase. Unemployment went down from around 16% to around 13% and stayed at that level in 1978 and 1979, column (4).[4]

The balance of payments was subject to contradictory forces during this phase. In 1976 it showed a surplus in spite of the negative effect of revaluation on the trade accounts: the depressed demand for imports predominated and was helped by an increasing inflow of foreign loans in such a way that a balance of payments surplus was generated. In the last two quarters of 1977, the situation was reversed due to the accumulated effect of two revaluations plus a higher demand for imports originating in the expansion of domestic production. A fall in copper prices of 13% with respect to the first two quarters of 1977 added to the forces that created a current account deficit of $500 million in 1977. To counteract the tendency, the exchange rate was devalued twice (in September and December 1977), and again in 1978. Given the program of tariff reductions and the compensating effect of devaluations, the cost of imports did not change much in the period. External inflows of capital accelerated, facilitating the accumulation of reserves, as column (2) shows. The high level of reserves by mid-1979 made possible the transition to phase 4.

Phase 4: Monetarism for the Open Economy Since June 1979

This phase corresponded to a stage when tariff reductions were completed. No import duties were above 10%, except for cars. Reserves were increasing, the fiscal deficit

4. Notice that these unemployment figures correspond to Greater Santiago only. Also, they do not include the unemployed absorbed in the Minimum Employment Program (PEM). National unemployment figures including and excluding PEM are given in Table 7.

had all but disappeared, and the economy continued giving signs of recuperating from the recession. At this point, in June 1979, the exchange rate was first devalued 5.7% and then fixed. Given that the economy was now open to international trade, it was hoped that the rate of price increases in the world economy would automatically regulate domestic inflation. After a lag, the latter should approach the former. When this happened, there was no need for further adjustments in the exchange rate. Global monetarism provided full automaticity to adjustment mechanisms in the economy.

Results in this phase were illustrative of the way automatic adjustment operated in practice. A fixed exchange rate plus the elimination of the fiscal deficit worked in favor of a reduction in the rate of inflation to 1.6% in the last quarter of 1981. On the other hand, for two and a half years starting in June 1979 domestic inflation was consistently above world inflation. The practical consequence of this, given a fixed nominal exchange rate, was that the real exchange rate appreciated by almost 30% in the period (from the second quarter in 1979 to the third quarter in 1981), column (6). The loss of competitiveness implied by this figure resulted in rapidly expanding trade and current accounts deficits that were to be equivalent to 10.7% and 15.1% of GDP by the end of 1981. The deficit resulted in a loss of reserves, in reduced capital inflows, and in sharp increases in the yearly rate of interest, which went up to almost 50% in real terms during the last quarter of 1981, column (12).

High interest rates and loss of competitiveness were responsible for a deep recession that began in the fourth quarter of 1980. A year later, industrial production was falling at a rate of 8% for the year when quarterly figures are compared. At the same time, unemployment went up once again. It reached 13.5% of the labor force in Santiago and 12.4% nationally. But if those employed in the Minimum Employment Program are included (earning less than $30 a month), national unemployment reached 17% in September 1981 and deteriorated even more thereafter. Recession, accompanied by a reduced inflow of external loans, high interest rates, and high indebtedness on the part of most firms, increased bankruptcies and bank failures. The government was forced to take over four banks and four financial companies on the verge of collapse. A deep financial crisis overtook most of the productive sector. After three years, the "miracle" seemed to be running out of steam.

Structural Changes

Having examined the course of short-term stabilization policies, let us now evaluate three of the long-term policy changes in the Chilean economy since 1973: privatization of the economy, opening up to trade, and changes in the composition of production and distribution of income.

Privatization

One of the basic elements of the new economic policy consisted in a drastic change in the role assigned to economic agents in Chile. The state gradually decreased in importance by means of a reduction in public expenditures and a more limited presence of the state as as producer and as a developmental agent.

As can be seen in Table 9, fiscal expenditures as a proportion of GDP dropped from 25.8 % in 1974 to 19.7 % in 1979. This was accompanied by a policy of privatization of public enterprises, which meant that out of 507 public enterprises in 1973, only fifteen remained in government hands by 1980 (shown in Table 10.) The state also diminished its developmental role, an outstanding characteristic of its action since the creation of the "Corporación de Fomento" (CORFO). This developmental role had increased considerably during the governments of Frei

TABLE 9 Fiscal Expenditures and Fiscal Deficit (percentages of GDP)	Year	Total Expenditures Excluding Public Debt	Fiscal Deficit
	1970	22.7	2.9
	1971	27.1	9.3
	1972	29.1	12.2
	1973	40.8	27.7
	1974	25.8	8.9
	1975	19.4	2.9
	1976	17.6	2.0
	1977	18.6	1.5
	1978	19.7	0.8

Sources:
Treasury Department, *Exposición sobre el Estado de la Hacienda Pública,* Jan. 1978, annual variation rates; and ODEPLAN, *Informe Gemines,* No. 21, 1979.

TABLE 10
Public Enterprises
(number of enterprises)

	1970	1973	1977	Target 1980
With participation in ownership				
Enterprises	46	229	45	15
Banks	—	19	4	—
Intervened enterprises	—	259	4	—
Enterprises in liquidation	—	—	17	—
Total	46	507	70	15

Sources:
CORFO, *Gerencia de Normalización,* 1979; and *El Mercurio* (Santiago), Feb. 27, 1980. The figures correspond to firms owned by CORFO.

and Allende, as can be seen from the figures of public employment by activity in Table 11. The withdrawal of the state from development assistance affected mainly small producers in the agricultural, mining, and industrial sectors as well as the process of agrarian reform, which not only came to a stop but was in fact reversed by returning a significant share of expropriated land to old owners, as will be seen later. Where the state left the field, the private sector—either domestic or foreign—entered.

TABLE 11

Employment in the Public Sector

(thousands of persons and annual variation rates, percentages)

	Administrative Services	Development Institutions	Social Services	Public Enterprises	Total
1964	32.3	28.5	49.6	49.6	209.9
1970	46.1	44.3	133.8	55.8	280.0
1974	52.8	69.5	178.3	59.5	360.2
1978	46.2	34.4	176.9	35.9	293.3
1979	48.8	32.0	176.3	35.5	292.6
Yearly growth rates 1964–1970	6.1	7.6	6.0	2.0	4.9
Yearly growth rates 1970–1974	3.5	11.9	7.4	1.6	6.5
Yearly growth rates 1974–1978	−3.3	−16.1	−0.2	−11.9	−5.0

Sources:
Finance Ministry, *Exposición sobre el Estado de la Hacienda Pública,* Jan. 1978, except for 1979 figures, which were obtained from J. Marshall and P. Romaguera, "Empleo en el sector público," CIEPLAN (mimeo), 1981.

TABLE 12
Financial Savings in Public and Private Institutions
(percentage of total)

	1969	1970	1974	1975	1976	1977	1978	1979
Public Sector	46.7	49.3	30.0	29.7	33.6	31.4	28.7	31.8
Central bank certificates	6.2	7.7	5.3	5.1	11.9	8.0	6.9	4.1
Public housing Corp.	3.3	3.2	0.8	0.9	0.6	0.6	0.5	0.2
Treasury bills	—	—	6.0	10.0	8.2	9.1	10.1	16.9
Reconstruction bonds	—	—	1.3	0.7	0.6	0.4	0.2	—
Savings, state bank	37.2	38.4	16.6	13.0	12.3	13.3	11.0	10.6
Mixed Sector (savings and loans)	40.5	39.5	62.5	56.2	36.1	17.8	7.8	3.5
Private Sector	12.8	11.1	7.5	14.1	40.3	50.9	63.5	64.7
Savings, commercial banks	11.5	9.8	1.6	9.0	26.2	40.2	50.7	46.9
Savings, development banks	1.3	1.3	0.1	2.3	0.7	1.8	4.0	7.1
Savings, financing institutions	—	—	5.8	2.8	3.4	8.9	8.8	10.7
Total	100.0	100.0	100.0	100.0	100.0	100.0	100.0	100.0

Source: Central Bank of Chile, *Boletín Mensual* (several issues).

Particularly important is the growth of private financial institutions. Table 12 shows that financial resources deposited in public institutions decreased from 49.3% of the total in 1970 to 31.8% in 1979. The share of the private sector increased from 11.1% in 1970 to 64.7% in 1979. Finally, the state diminished its role as regulator of external flows. The tax treatment for foreign investment was liberalized. Restrictions on the remittances of profits abroad were eliminated, and the ceiling on external borrowing by the private sector was gradually lifted.[5]

This withdrawal of the state from economic activity was accompanied by a substantial decrease in public employment, as shown in Table 11. Public sector employment fell by 21% between 1974 and 1978. Thus, previous expansionary trends were drastically reversed.[6] The employment reductions are more important in development institutions (19% reduction per year) and in public enterprises (10.5% reduction per year). These figures reflect the priorities in the new economic policy.

Organized labor is excluded from this picture. Not only were wages controlled and in fact drastically curtailed in real terms, but no collective bargaining was allowed, strikes were forbidden, and no mechanism existed for the participation of labor in economic decisions. Only in 1979 was a "Labor Plan" implemented, which regulated, under conditions of subordination of workers to the employers, the functioning of labor unions and allowed for a very restricted form of collective bargaining, as will be seen in the next chapter.

The changes in the role of economic agents, which we have just described (less state participation, privatization of economic activities, modifications in labor legislation), was initially posed only as an efficiency requirement of the model. It

5. J. E. Herrera and J. Morales, "La inversión financiera externa: El caso de Chile 1974–1978," *Colección Estudios CIEPLAN*, No. 1, 1979.
6. With regard to 1973, public employment dropped 25% and represented a decrease of 100,000 persons.

TABLE 13

Subsidy in the Sale of State Enterprises*
(millions of dollars in 1978)

Discount Rate		Sale Value	Value of Assets in 1978	Subsidy	Subsidy as % of Asset Value
1974– 1978	1979– 1983				
10	10	496.1	731.8	235.7	32.2
25	15	533.0	731.8	198.8	27.2

*The figures correspond to a sample of forty-one enterprises and banks, which represent around 60% of the firms auctioned. The value of the sale updated to 1978 assumed a four-year payment period for the industrial firms and eight quarters for banks, with interest rates of 10% and 8%, respectively.

Sources:
E. Dahse, *Mapa de la extrema riqueza* (Editorial Aconcagua, Santiago, 1979); and CORFO, *Gerencia de Normalización,* 1979.

was supposedly neutral as to its distributive effects. In practice this was not so. In fact, the economy's adjustment process to the desired conditions implied a massive transfer of resources toward the private sector, particularly toward financial firms and large industrial enterprises. This transfer of resources was made possible because of the particular form taken by the processes of privatization, market liberalization, and inflationary control.

Thus, privatization of state enterprises occurred in extremely advantageous conditions for the new owners. In Table 13 we have estimated the implicit subsidy for those who bought these public assets. The subsidy, calculated on the basis of the market value of assets, turned out to be equivalent to 30% of the firms' net worth and up to 40% and 50% of the purchase value.[7] The low sale price was influenced by the state's urgency

7. The calculation was made based on the figures of E. Dahse, *Mapa de la extrema riqueza* (Editorial Aconcagua, Santiago, 1979), for a sample of forty-one enterprises, as explained in the note in Table 13.

TABLE 14

Balance of the Agrarian Reform in April 1979

Situation	Hectares	Percentage
Restitution to former owners	2,965,640	29.8
Area assigned*	3,521,141	35.3
Transfers to CORA**	1,639,772	16.5
In the hands of ODENA†	1,839,315	18.4
Total expropriated	9,965,868	100.0

*From the total of the area assigned to the beneficiaries of agrarian reform up to June 1978, almost 40% had been sold or leased for its exploitation to third parties.

**Land Reform Corporation; includes auction of lands and transfers to other public institutions (such as CONAF, National Forestry Corporation) or to private ones.

†Office of Agricultural Normalization.

Source:
Presentation of the government of Chile to the Conference on Agrarian Reform and Rural Development, 1979, in Comentarios sobre la situación económica, Department of Economics, University of Chile, 1st semester, 1979.

to sell and its doing so in a moment of deep recession and high interest rates, a point at which short-term profitability of the enterprises decreased. Given these circumstances, only those firms which had liquid resources or access to cheap foreign credit were in a position to buy the auctioned enterprises.

Something similar occurred in the agricultural sector, in which the policy was to return a fraction of the lands expropriated during the agrarian reform to their original owners. Another part was subdivided into individual plots and handed over to peasants (see Table 14). In April 1979, 30% of the expropriated land had been returned to the former owners, and 35% had been assigned in individual plots to peasants and small farmers. Moreover, already in June 1978, nearly 40% of these lands had been sold or leased by peasants to third parties, as a consequence of the high cost of credit and reduced technical assistance.

The privatization of manufacturing firms, as well as that of the land reform sector, implied a transfer of assets, generally undervalued, either to former owners in the agricultural case or to business groups in the industrial and financial sectors. The foregoing tendency was reinforced by the particular form taken by the process of market liberalization. Thus, the liberalization of the foreign credit market was only partial. A ceiling was imposed on foreign borrowing as a percentage of the value of assets. Given that only large enterprises and the better established banks and financial institutions had access to cheap, rationed external credit and that domestic interest rates were much higher, this constituted a source of large profits for banks and larger firms. Zahler has estimated the profit for the enterprises that had access to external credit in the period 1976–1979 to be in the order of $800 million.[8] These profits arose from the high differential in interest rates, taking into account expected devaluation between the foreign rates (from 6% to 11%) and domestic interest rates in dollars (between 118% and 42%).

On the other hand, the process of market liberalization did not follow uniform rules with regard to factor and goods prices. Upon the drastic freeing up of prices followed by wage contraction, a strong bias against labor set in (see Table 15). There was a drastic fall of the relative price of labor with respect to wholesale, export, and industrial prices (see Table 15). The relative reduction in wages reached between 50% and 60% on 1976 and was still between 25–40% during 1978.

These sets of relative prices are extremely favorable to productive enterprises, particularly those in export activities. Undoubtedly it allowed them to absorb a good part of the greater costs associated with the severe 1975–1976 recession, and it provided a cushion that facilitated adjustment to increased ex-

8. R. Zahler, "Repercusiones monetarias y reales de la apertura de la economía chilena 1975–1978," *Revista de la CEPAL,* April 1980.

ternal competition resulting from lower tariffs. The effect of changes in relative prices was reinforced when considering the reduction in the employer's contribution to social security. The accumulated effect of both factors on the cost of labor can be observed in column (2) of Table 16. Given labor productivity increases, the incidence of labor costs for the industrial producer dropped from 15.8% of the gross value of production in 1970 to 9.6% in 1979, column (4).

Another important way in which resources were transferred to large business firms came about as a by-product of the policy of economic stabilization. This policy was characterized by a strict monetarist, closed economy approach, at least until mid-1979. The policy sought economic stabilization through

TABLE 15

Prices and Wages
(1970 indexes=100)

	Remunerations ÷ Wholesale Prices (1)	Remunerations ÷ Export Prices (2)	Industrial Remunerations ÷ Industrial Prices (3)
1970	100.0	100.0	100.0
1974	49.6	50.4	57.2
1975	38.9	35.2	47.9
1976	41.3	45.5	56.0
1977	52.6	59.5	69.0
1978	57.9	57.2	75.0
1979	56.6	63.7	74.9
1980	59.3	80.0	79.6

Sources:

(1) INE, Indice de Sueldos y Salarios (Index of Wages and Salaries—ISS); and Wholesale Price Index, national products.

(2) INE, ISS, exchange rate; and R.

Ffrench-Davis, "Indice de precios externos y valor real del comercio internacional de Chile," Notas Técnicas, No. 15, CIEPLAN, 1979.

(3) INE, ISS, industrial sector and industrial Wholesale Price Index.

TABLE 16

Productivity and Labor Costs
in the Industrial Sector
(percentages)

Year	Wages (1)	Cost of Labor (2)	Physical Productivity (3)	Cost of Labor Over GVP* (4)
1970	100.0	100.0	100.0	15.8
1974	57.2	61.2	103.5	9.4
1975	47.9	49.4	79.5	9.8
1976	56.0	57.7	93.9	9.7
1977	69.0	69.6	104.4	10.5
1978	75.0	71.1	109.5	10.3
1979	74.9	69.2	113.0	9.6

*Gross Value of Production.

Sources:

(1) INE, *Indice de Sueldos y Salarios;* industrial sector and industrial Wholesale Price Index.

(2) Column (1) plus the employer's contribution to social security. The actual rate of contribution effective for 1974 was considered, as calculated by ODEPLAN, *Cuentas Nacionales de Chile* (old National Accounts), and it was varied for the following years according to the rates of the service of social security.

(3) Ibid.; and employment by sectors; figures from ibid.

(4) For 1970 ibid.; for the following years it is calculated using columns (2) and (3).

partial use of the instruments at its disposal, principally the reduction of real cash balances, real wages, and the fiscal deficit.

The approach was successful in producing a sharp drop in effective demand and in reducing real wages. Prices increased without relation to demand since the impact of expectations and costs was difficult to gauge in a situation which passed rapidly from "repressed" inflation to open inflation. Consequently, high inflation continued far longer than expected.[9]

9. See J. Ramos, "The Economics of Hyperstagflation," *Journal of Development Economics,* Dec. 1980.

The economy entered a prolonged phase of recession with high inflation, a period characterized by generalized market disequilibrium. Market imbalances surfaced in the form of sharp and intermittent movements in relative prices. Anyone with enough liquidity to react quickly to these fluctuations in relative prices benefited from those movements. So did, obviously, anyone with special access to economic information that allowed him correctly to predict those movements or to know ahead of time of any corrective measures planned by the government.

The economic groups which controlled the country's large firms and financial sector took full advantage of these opportunities for speculation. Market disequilibria and high inflation lasted over five years, long enough for those groups to corner for themselves the speculative gains available in different markets.

In short, beginning in 1973, the operation of the Chilean economy fundamentally changed not only because the economic roles assigned to different participants changed but also because the dynamic processes of adjustment to a new economic model made possible the real transfer of resources toward industrial-financial groups. These groups took advantage of this resource transfer, using it to acquire a dominant position in the country's productive apparatus, as will be shown below.

Transition from a Closed to an Open Economy

At the end of 1973, the average nominal tariff on imports to Chile was 94%. By June 1979, a gradual policy of tariff reductions brought nearly all tariffs down to a uniform 10% except for automotive vehicles. The process of tariff reduction, which took a little over five years, was part of a general liberalization of restrictions on foreign trade: elimination of nontariff barriers and a reduction on limits to foreign investment, foreign credit, and foreign exchange transactions. At the same time, however, the government attempted to maintain an exchange rate that would favor Chilean exports. The government also sought to encourage exports by exempting exported goods from the across-the-board value-added tax on all products sold in Chile and from export custom duties.

Policies designed to open the economy were resolutely put into effect from 1974 to 1978. By the end of six years, the Chilean economy was well on its way to becoming an "open" economy with few barriers to international trade. We will review briefly the principal changes that have occurred as a result of the transition from a closed to an open economy.[10]

One of the objectives of liberalizing imports was to encourage the development of an export sector. Lower tariffs reduced the cost to the Chilean producer of intermediate goods. An increase in the volume of imports raised the equilibrium exchange rate for the dollar, creating an exchange rate more favorable to export growth.

The policy of export stimulation was helped by the low wage rates which prevailed during that period, as was shown in Tables 7 and 8, and by the special tax exemptions on exports mentioned above. The policy was also aided by excess capacity in the industrial sector, which resulted from the anti-inflation program.

The growth of exports in the period was undoubtedly significant. Normalizing for the price of copper, total exports rose from 15% of GDP in 1970 to 18% in 1977. Nevertheless, the greater success was obtained in the growth of nontraditional exports, as shown in Table 17. During the period 1974–1979, nontraditional exports tripled. This was accompanied by export diversification. If copper is excluded from total exports to avoid the effect of excessive price fluctuations, industrial exports rose from 59% of total exports in 1974 (excluding copper) to 65% in 1978.

10. What follows is based on studies by R. Ffrench-Davis, "Políticas de comercio exterior en Chile 1973–1978," CIEPLAN (mimeo), Santiago, 1979; and P. Vergara, "Apertura externa y desarrollo industrial en Chile 1974–1978," *Colección Estudios CIEPLAN,* No. 4, 1980.

TABLE 17

Imports and Exports
(in millions of dollars in 1977)

	1970	1974	1978	1979	1980
Imports					
Food consumption goods	110.5	85.9	117.0	133.1	297.5
Non-food consumption goods	189.8	237.9	415.3	540.7	752.5
Capital goods	566.0	337.9	573.2	683.9	857.2
Intermediate goods	1,085.5	1,778.3	1,594.0	1,969.8	2,186.0
Total	1,951.8	2,440.0	2,699.5	3,327.5	4,093.2
Exports					
Traditional	1,951.4	2,268.0	1,250.1	1,757.7	2,041.2
Semitraditional	95.9	175.4	230.0	300.0	360.8
Nontraditional	232.4	274.5	650.7	894.0	986.2
Total	2,279.7	2,717.9	2,130.8	2,951.7	3,388.2

Source:
R. Ffrench-Davis, "Liberalización chilena en 1973–1979," *Colección de importaciones: La experiencia Estudios CIEPLAN,* No. 4, 1980.

As regards imports, they grew rapidly after 1978, as seen in Table 17. The expansion is particularly significant for imports of nonfood consumption goods, which more than doubled between 1974 and 1979. On the other hand, imports of capital goods fell during the recession, and only in 1978 did they recuperate 1970 levels.

What impact had the opening up of the economy on the structure of production, particularly in the industrial sector? The manufacturing sector suffered the simultaneous impact of recession and tariff reduction, which negatively affected production levels. Both effects are not easy to separate. Yet, based on the study by Vergara, we have grouped in Table 18 sectoral data that will allow us to distinguish among sectors depending on how they had been affected by the opening up to trade and by recession, respectively. In group A in Table 18 we have classified those sectors that were simultaneously affected by falls in domestic demand and by tariff reduction. In these sectors production decreased and imports increased, giving way to a marked desubstitution of imports. Therefore, this is a case of sectors which have been affected simultaneously by falls in demand and by import liberalization. This group includes textiles, shoes, and clothing, as well as some intermediate inputs for industry. Group B includes those activities in which, in spite of an increase in domestic demand, production fell. At the same time, imports increased significantly. These are sectors typically affected by the opening up to trade. This group includes the electronics industry and transport, among others. Group C consists of intermediate inputs for construction and rubber and plastics. These sectors are mainly affected by recession rather than by tariff reduction. This may be verified by observing that in the face of contractions in demand, both imports and production decreased, but the former fell even more sharply. Group D represents export-oriented activities that successfully adjusted to lower tariffs, like wood and paper. In group E, whose principal component is food, beverages, and tobacco, we have included sectors where both production and imports grew.

Table 19 shows the behavior of employment by branches of industry. The sectors most affected were textiles, clothing, and footwear and metallic products, machinery, and equipment. These are activities in which the negative impact of recession and opening up to trade are probably reinforced, as we saw before. Other sectors similarly affected were nonmetallic minerals and basic metals, which typically depend on domestic intermediate demand, particularly of investment goods. Investment remained at low levels throughout the period.

It is interesting to note that for all industrial sectors, except wood and paper, an additional deterioration in employment was produced after the recession was over, that is, after 1976, which was a period when tariff reduction had the strongest impact. This indicates that the declines in industrial employment cannot be explained as only a transitional result of reces-

TABLE 18

Opening up to World Markets: Effects on the Industrial Sector
(annual variation rates 1969/70–1978, percentages)

	Production (1)	Imports (2)	Exports (3)	Domestic Demand (4)	Import Substitution (5)
A. *Affected by opening and fall of internal demand*	-2.5	4.7	22.6	-1.8	-11.2
Textiles, clothing and footwear (321, 322, 323, and 324)*	-0.6	6.1	46.0	-1.2	-3.4
Industrial inputs (351, 354, 361, and 382)	-5.9	4.8	24.2	-3.3	-22.2
Others (342 and 385)	-2.2	2.8	-7.4	-0.6	-9.1
B. *Affected by Opening up to Trade*	-1.1	8.7	23.3	2.0	-17.7
Electronic equipment (3832)	-1.1	14.0	-15.4	6.7	-27.2
Transportation material (384)	-1.2	6.9	46.5	2.2	-14.4
C. *Affected by the Fall in Internal Demand*	-1.6	-7.0	5.8	-3.0	8.0
Intermediate for construction (369, 371, and 381)	-1.5	-6.0	12.9	-2.9	6.7
Unvulcanized rubber and plastics (355 and 356)	-1.9	-16.4	-8.7	-3.6	13.2
D. *Oriented to Exports*	*2.9*	*-9.2*	*11.4*	*-0.7*	*6.4*
Timber (331)	4.4	-29.9	15.4	2.9	11.4
Paper (341)	0.6	2.4	10.0	-8.5	-2.0
E. *Others* (311, 312, 313, 314, 352, 362, 383, and 390)	*2.1*	*4.8*	*17.1*	*1.7*	*-1.4*
F. *Total*	*0.2*	*1.6*	*15.3*	*-0.6*	*-1.4*

*Figures in parentheses identify branches according to the International Standard Classification of Industry by the United Nations.

Source:
P. Vergara, "Apertura externa y desarrollo industrial en Chile 1974–1978," *Colección Estudios CIE-PLAN*, No. 4, 1980. Domestic demand is measured as a proxy by the difference between production plus imports minus exports. Column (5) indicates the variation in the import coefficient over total supply. No figures with this sectoral breakdown are available after 1978.

sion. The ongoing change in the industrial structure seemed to be generating a lower demand for labor. Whether this was only a transitory phenomenon typical of the adjustment process or a more permanent one is something that cannot be answered with the available evidence.

In brief, empirical evidence indicates that trade liberalization caused: (1) significant export expansion, (2) a change in the composition of imports in which the most rapid growth was observed in the imports of nonfood consumption goods, (3) a differentiated impact of tariff reduction on the various branches of industry, and (4) stagnation in industrial employment, accompanied by a slow recuperation in industrial output levels. Undoubtedly this adjustment process was helped by the

TABLE 19

Industrial Production and Employment

(1970 indexes = 100)

	1970	1974	1976	1978
EMPLOYMENT	*100*	*110.4*	*92.6*	*92.0*
Foods, drinks, and tobacco	100	107.0	103.4	99.1
Textiles, clothing, and footwear	100	109.9	87.1	87.6
Timber	100	99.5	72.2	99.3
Paper	100	109.3	98.0	94.5
Chemicals	100	114.1	102.3	98.5
Nonmetallic minerals	100	117.4	91.6	86.0
Basic metallic	100	112.6	101.3	88.9
Metallic products, machinery, and equipment	100	117.8	92.0	84.3
PRODUCTION				
INE	100	108.6	81.9	96.3
SOFOFA	100	107.3	92.2	110.9

Sources:
SOFOFA, *Indice de Producción y Ocupación Industrial,* 1979; and INE, *Indice de Producción Industrial,* 1979.

remarkable fall in wages with respect to the exchange rate and to industrial prices, as was seen in Table 15.

By these means, the industrial sector was able to absorb part of the impact of increased external competition. There is also some evidence that firms hedged against foreign competition by becoming importers of competitive products.[11] On the other hand, a greater specialization in production was evident in some industries as a way of increasing production efficiency in order to meet the import challenge.[12] Another factor which facilitated the adjustment was the access to foreign loans. The flow of foreign credits to the private sector increased sharply, as was seen in Table 5.

It is perhaps too early to make a definite assessment of the impact of trade liberalization in Chile. Although the process of tariff reduction ended in 1979, the appreciation of domestic currency that resulted from a fixed exchange rate established in June 1979 (given that domestic inflation more than doubled external inflation at the time) was further reducing effective protection in the industrial sector. A final evaluation must wait until these effects have sorted themselves out.

Changes in the
Composition of Production

Up to this point, we have analyzed the main changes in the economy which resulted from policy reforms begun in 1973. These changes, the new roles of participants in the economy, and the greater degree of openness to foreign trade no doubt have repercussions on the structure of production and on patterns of income and wealth distribution. But the effects are slow to take form. Given the short period of time which has passed, we can now only observe the emerging outlines of some of the tendencies.

Table 20 shows the composition of production and employment for the principal productive sectors. The primary sec-

11. Ffrench-Davis, "Políticas de comercio exterior."
12. Vergara, "Apertura externa."

tors (agriculture and mining) increased their relative importance in production from 20% in 1970 to 22% in 1978. In spite of its greater importance in production, the participation of the primary sectors in employment fell from 26% in 1970 to 22.7% in 1978.

On the other hand, the manufacturing sector dropped its relative importance in GDP, as would be expected, since it was the most heavily protected sector before the tariff reforms and was at the same time affected by reductions in domestic demand. The industrial sector participation in GDP fell three percentage points between 1970 and 1978. In employment, the reduction was close to two percentage points. The reduction of industrial employment continued as a tendency even after 1976 when the industrial product began to recuperate.

The most dynamic sectors in the period were commerce and service. Jointly considered, their participation in production rose from 42% in 1970 to 45% in 1978. One out of two jobs in the economy was generated in these sectors toward 1978.[13] The importance acquired by the service sectors was such that their participation in product and employment was higher than that of all productive sectors jointly considered (agriculture, mining, and industry). On the other hand, infrastructure and construction activities decreased in importance. The latter reduced its participation in the product by half.

In sum, the changes in the structure of production and employment were meaningful in spite of the short time that transpired. A part of these changes do not reflect modifications in the productive capacity but only in the degree of utilization of that capacity.[14] The direction of the changes is clear: the pro-

13. This happens in spite of the fact that employment in education and health was reduced. The employment in other services instead increased by 21% between 1975 and 1977.

14. Of course, to the extent that idle capacity is maintained as such for an extended period in some sectors, it may become a signal for further expansions to be oriented toward other activities, those where the "new" demand is concentrated.

TABLE 20

Production Composition and Employment
(percentages)

	1970		1974		1978	
	Production	Employment	Production	Employment	Production*	Employment**
Agriculture	9.7	22.6	9.1	18.3	10.2	19.3
Mining	10.7	3.2	11.6	3.7	12.0	3.4
Industry	26.0	17.8	25.7	18.5	22.7	16.1
Construction	5.0	6.9	4.8	5.7	2.8	4.0
Energy and transportation	6.4	7.4	6.8	7.6	7.1	7.3
Commerce (trade)	22.3	12.1	21.9	12.7	23.6	16.7
Services†	19.9	30.0	20.1	33.4	21.6	33.3
Total	100.0	100.0	100.0	100.0	100.0	100.0

*Corresponds to the employment survey of 1975; there is no information for 1974.

**Corresponds to the employment survey of 1977; last information available.

†Excludes housing property.

Sources:
The production columns come from ODEPLAN, *Cuentas Nacionales de Chile*; the employment columns come from ODEPLAN, *Antecedentes sobre el desarrollo económico chileno*, 1960–1970.

duction of commerce and services grew at a significant rate. Industry and the sectors of infrastructure grew at a very slow pace. These unbalances in sectoral growth, if persistent, will probably end up modifying permanently not only the productive structure but also income distribution patterns.

Changes in Patterns of Distribution

An economy which undergoes profound changes such as Chile experienced beginning in 1973 will probably, in the long run, sustain changes not only in its production and trade structure but also in its patterns of distribution. Some of the important factors related to changes in income distribution are changes in patterns of property ownership, in the relative power of different participants in the economy, and in the importance of different productive sectors.

What has happened to the first two of these factors in the period we are studying? We have described earlier how the roles of the economic participants changed as a result of the reduction of the role of the state and the rapid privatization of economic activities. This process and the government's general policy orientation favored privileged participation and access to resources by the business sector, particularly by large and medium-sized firms and by the financial sector. These were the sectors which most benefited from the massive transfer of resources that accompanied the transition from high inflation and a closed economy to more moderate prices and an "open"economy.

A recent study identifies the groups that benefited from this process and describes the concentration of wealth that resulted from it. By the end of 1978, five economic conglomerates controlled 53% of the total assets of Chile's 250 largest private enterprises. Nine conglomerates, including these five, controlled 82% of the assets in the Chilean banking system. These nine groups also controlled 60%of total bank credits and 64%

TABLE 21

Employment and Unemployment
(thousands of persons)

	Labor Force (1)	Employed (2)	Unemployed (3)	Unemployment Rate (4)	PEM* (5)	Unemployment plus PEM on Labor Force (6)
1970	2,950.1	2,770.1	180.0	6.1	—	6.1
1974	3,112.2	2,925.9	286.3	9.2	—	9.2
1975	3,112.0	2,703.7	418.3	13.4	60.6	15.3
1976	3,187.9	2,674.6	513.3	16.1	157.8	21.1
1977	3,231.5	2,772.6	458.9	14.2	187.7	20.0
1978	3,329.3	2,856.5	472.8	14.2	145.8	18.6
1979	3,442.1	2,967.1	475.0	13.8	133.9	17.7
1980**	3,529.6	3,088.8	440.8	12.5	190.7	17.9

*Minimum Employment Program.

**Figures for 1980 are preliminary official statistics, which are questionable. They assume a 5% rate of growth for the labor force between the second and fourth quarters of 1980. The historical trend gives a 2% yearly growth rate for the labor force.

Sources:

Columns (1) to (4) are based on the methodology developed by P. Meller, R. Cortázar, and J. Marshall, *Colección Estudios CIEPLAN*, No. 2, Santiago, 1979. This methodology was applied to INE data.

Column (5): INE *Informativo Estadístico.*

Column (6) was obtained from columns (1), (3), and (5).

of loans made by financial institutions. The same study showed that in a sample of 100 enterprises, the assets of firms controlled by the five most important conglomerates seemed to grow 97% between 1969 and 1978 while assets of the remaining firms grew only 14%. These figures are indicative of the rapid expansion of conglomerates, a significant feature in the process of asset concentration, together with the privatizations, the reversion of agrarian reform, and the liberalization of prices accompanied by wage repression.[15]

In the short term, that is, until 1978, the distributive changes were strongly influenced by the high unemployment rates and the fall of real wages (see Table 21).[16] Employment at a national level, which had grown 2% per year in the 1960s, showed a growth of only 0.7% per year between 1974 and 1980.

The slow growth of employment together with an expansion of the working age population of 14% between 1974 and 1980 explains the high unemployment rates observed, which are more than twice the historic rates. In 1980 unemployment reached 11.8%. Adding the Minimum Employment Program, the figure would rise to 17.2%. The unemployment rate for blue-collar workers reached 28.4% if one includes the Minimum Employment Program.[17] High unemployment was accompanied by a fall in real wages, which reached 40% at the end of 1974 and early 1975.[18]

15. Dahse, *Mapa de la extrema riqueza.*

16. Employment figures rectify previous official estimates that showed a rapid expansion in employment. New figures are from a study by P. Meller, R. Cortázar, and J. Marshall, *Colección Estudios CIEPLAN,* No. 2, Santiago, 1979.

17. This figure is for 1977, the last year in which this information was available. See INE, *Encuesta Nacional del Empleo* (Santiago, 1977).

18. It must be noted that the index of wages and salaries that was utilized underestimated the actual wage reduction in the economy as a whole. The index represented adequately only the average wages and salaries in industrial firms with more than twenty employees and in mining and services sectors, in which wages and salaries were lower. See University of Chile, Department of Economics, *Comentarios sobre la situación económica,* 2nd semester, 1978.

TABLE 22   Distribution of Household Consumption
by Quintiles: Greater Santiago, Chile (percentages)

		Share of Total Consumption	
	Quintiles	1969	1978
	I	7.7	5.2
	II	12.1	9.3
Sources:	III	16.0	13.6
INE, *Encuesta de Presupuestos Familiares,* 1969; and INE, *Encuesta de Presupuestos Familiares,* 1978.	IV	21.0	20.9
	V	43.2	51.0
	Total	100.0	100.0

The simultaneous reduction in employment and wages generated a regressive distribution of income, a proxy for which we consider household consumption expenditures by income brackets. The figures in Table 22 point to a concentration of consumption in the high-income brackets.[19]

On the other hand, empirical evidence shows a marked stratification in consumption. The consumption of nonessential imported consumer goods, which grew about 300% between 1970 and 1978, was highly concentrated in the highest 20% of families. These families consumed nearly 60% of the total (see Table 23). The trickle-down in consumption to other income groups was scarce, being almost negligible for the lower 20% of the families.

19. This information, which is in accord with wages and employment data, contradicted official statements that the income distribution in 1978 would not be significantly different from that in 1970. According to a study by I. Heskia, the distribution improved even in the worst recession years. For a criticism of Heskia's results, see R. Cortázar, "Remuneraciones, empleo y distribución del ingreso en Chile 1970–1978," *Colección Estudios CIEPLAN,* No. 3, 1980. See I. Heskia, "Distribución del ingreso en el Gran Santiago 1957–1978," *Documento de Investigación,* No. 41, Economics Department, University of Chile, Santiago, 1979.

In contrast with the expansion of luxury consumption, which concentrated in high-income groups, essential food consumption per family for the poorer groups showed a reduction of 20% in real terms between 1969 and 1978 (see Table 24). Instead, the consumption per family of the same basic food products for the high-income groups grew slightly. This marked dualism in consumption seems to be an essential characteristic of the model. It is in agreement with the patrimonial changes and with the income distribution patterns previously discussed.

An Overall View
of Economic Performance

The Chilean economy in the period under study has simultaneously been subject to a process of economic stabilization and a transition toward a free market economy. In the first aspect a substantial decrease in the rate of inflation was attained; the balance of payments was adjusted, accumulating international reserves; and, after passing through a deep recession, the economy showed signs of recuperating 1970 production levels.

Other indicators, however, show negative results: high unemployment persisted in the seventh year of application of the policy, distribution of income and household expenditures was regressive, investment levels were low, and the deficit in the current account of the balance of payments was growing, as was the external debt. These indicators cast a shadow on the growth potential of the model, as has been applied in Chile, and in its capacity to absorb labor in productive activities.

But macroeconomic indicators are only the more visible, but perhaps less important, part of the revolutionary process of change in the Chilean economy during this period. The process of transition to a free market economy implied that, simultane-

TABLE 23   Imported Non-essential Consumption
(millions of dollars in 1977 and percentage of total consumption)

	IMPORTS			CONSUMPTION BY QUINTILES				
	1970	1978	Rate of Growth	High Incomes V	IV	III	II	Low Incomes I
Leather manufactures and furriers	1.3	3.4	161.5	69.2	16.9	8.6	4.0	1.3
Imported alcoholic drinks	0.6	11.9	1,883.0	54.8	5.0	0.0	0.2	0.0
Imported tobacco, cigarettes, and cigars	7.7	9.4	22.1	91.7	4.5	3.6	0.2	0.0
Clothing, textiles for the house, and carpets	24.1	91.0	277.6	55.0	21.1	12.9	8.0	3.0
Photographic and cinematographic products	7.8	10.3	32.1	62.6	14.8	22.0	0.6	0.0
Footwear, hats, umbrellas, and sunshades	2.0	7.3	265.0	41.6	24.2	17.3	11.2	5.7
Musical and optical instruments	4.3	9.6	123.3	59.6	20.3	13.5	5.5	1.1
Toys, games, and recreational articles	3.4	22.6	564.7	61.0	22.3	8.9	5.7	2.1
Cosmetics, eau de cologne, and perfumes	0.1	6.6	6,500.0	39.7	24.9	16.8	12.0	6.6
Black and white, and color TV sets (only color)	0.7	56.3	7,942.9	30.3 (100.0)	18.3 (0.0)	23.5 (0.0)	19.3 (0.0)	8.6 (0.0)
Radios (excluding portable radios)	4.6	28.7	523.9	48.7 (54.9)	21.5 (22.9)	14.6 (11.1)	12.5 (11.0)	2.7 (0.1)
Cars and motorcycles	19.0	40.6	113.7	97.4	2.6	0.0	0.0	0.0
Total	75.6	297.7	293.8	56.4	19.1	12.6	8.4	3.5

Sources: R. Ffrench-Davis, "Políticas de comercio exterior en Chile 1973–1978," CIEPLAN (mimeo), Santiago, 1979; and INE, *Encuesta de Presupuestos Familiares* 3 (May 1979).

ously with the anti-inflationary policy, deep structural reforms were carried out: a drastic privatization of the economy, a quick opening of the economy to world markets, and a massive transfer of resources to the modern sector of industry and finance. As a consequence of the last factor, powerful conglomerates with ample economic and political influence emerged. This was one of the outstanding traits of the industrial organization scheme that arose from the experiment.

The conglomerates or "economic groups" were, in fact, the new actors in the process of development. They increasingly controlled industrial assets, as well as that of banks and financial institutions. Besides, they were the dynamic agents in the process of industrial adjustment to face foreign competition. These conglomerates were the ones that related to international private banks and controlled the larger proportion in the flow of external loans.

The other basic modification in the functioning of the Chilean economy refers to the radical opening up to world markets. Although several industrial branches suffered significant losses in markets and industrial employment went down, some activities seemed to adapt successfully. This lasted until 1981, when external shocks and wrong policies submerged all industrial activities in a deep crisis.

The financial opening, which goes together with the commercial opening, helped to overcome the problems derived from the recession and the transition to the open economy. Nevertheless, it has had distorting effects in other respects. It prolonged the price stabilization period as it became the most important source of monetary expansion. At the same time, it reinforced the tendency toward asset concentration as it gave differentiated access to cheap external credit (in comparison with domestic credit) mainly to large enterprises of the modern sector and made it possible to keep an undervalued exchange rate that coexisted with large deficits in trade flows.

TABLE 24
Average Consumption of Basic Food Products by Household
(pesos in June 1978)

	Lower 20%			Higher 20%		
		Consumption			Consumption	
	1969	1978	Variation %	1969	1978	Variation %
Flours and starches	387.6	406.8	5.0	778.6	719.6	−7.6
Meats	357.9	219.1	−38.8	1,534.5	1,627.2	6.0
Oils	105.4	71.2	−32.4	269.4	201.0	−25.4
Dairy and new ones	138.9	106.1	−23.6	618.3	641.5	3.8
Vegetables and legumes	144.0	97.5	−32.3	257.9	197.4	−23.5
Sugar	97.0	73.4	−24.3	191.8	154.2	−19.6
Energy and fuel	227.3	181.8	−20.0	501.6	641.1	27.8
Urban transport	129.8	102.9	−20.7	277.8	284.5	2.4
Total	1,587.9	1,258.8	−20.7	4,430.0	4,466.5	0.8
% of total consumption		49.9			18.0	

Source: INE, Encuesta de Presupuestos Familiares, 1969 and 1978.

Production adjustment, as a result of the opening up of the economy, is just beginning to occur. As expected, initially production patterns were oriented toward expanding primary producing activites (mainly copper mining and agricultural and forestry products) and exports. The most dynamic sectors were commerce, financial activities, and personal services. The first two were stimulated by expanded foreign trade and by the development of the capital market. Demand for personal services grew as a consequence of the rapid expansion in income for high-income groups. At the same time that the productive structure changed, a higher degree of asset and income concentration was observed.

What type of economy emerged from the deep structural changes undertaken in Chile after 1973? It is too early to tell. In principle, what we have is an open economy, with more specialization and potentially higher incentives for efficiency in domestic production. It is also an economy that is more vulnerable with respect to changes, shocks, and fluctuations in the international economy. It is highly dependent on the availability of private external credit in order to balance the current account deficit.

A salient feature of the model is the wide divergence of income and consumption patterns between the rich and the rest of the population. With respect to consumption, a marked stratification is produced. The "deprivation horizon" is a reality for low-income groups, as is "the opulent consumer society" for the higher-income sectors.

This is only one of the unsolved problems. Other persistent problems are extremely high unemployment and low investment. In the political sphere the model has not been able to solve the inherent contradiction between economic freedom—a basic objective of the model and of the Friedmanian ideology—and the political authoritarianism which accompanies it, although efforts have been made to integrate these disparate elements in one common ideology. We shall explore this matter in more detail in the next chapter.

Postscript

As this book goes to press, my evaluation of results in Chapter 3 looks rather benign. During 1982, the Chilean economy entered into a deep crisis in productive and financial activities that threatened to undo the structural changes undertaken since 1973.

In June 1982, industrial production was falling at a yearly rate of 20%, unemployment was around 25%, bankruptcies had skyrocketed, and banks and financial companies exhibited a ratio of bad loans over capital and reserves well in excess of 50%, forcing the Central Bank to intervene, by indirect means, in the whole financial system. *Real* interest rates were around 50% a year. Capital inflows were decreasing. The loss of reserves between January and June 1982 (in the Central Bank and in private banks) amounted to $750 million, a 30% fall. The exchange rate had suffered a devaluation of more than 50%, and previous policies were being gradually abandoned.

What caused this serious crisis? As we have previously pointed out, by the end of 1981 the economy already exhibited a huge balance-of-payments current-account deficit. In fact, it reached 15% of GDP. This was a consequence of an economy excessively open to foreign competition, where the loss of competitiveness was caused by low tariffs (10%) reinforced by a fall of 30% in the real exchange rate between June 1979 and late 1981 (in June 1979 the nominal exchange rate was fixed). This was aggravated by an excess inflow of foreign capital between 1978 and 1981. Debt service over exports of goods and services for 1981 was 57%. And outstanding debt was approaching 50% of GDP. This caused capital inflows to decrease by the end of 1981, aggravating the productive and financial crisis.

The crisis was aggravated by the reliance of Chilean policymakers on an "automatic adjustment" of the economy, when these events made themselves present. Following the monetary approach to the balance of payments as a theoretical guideline, policymakers relied on endogenous corrections in money supply, induced by a loss of reserves, and in the subsequent increases in the rate of interest, as the mechanisms to "automatically" correct the balance of payments deficit. The latter was diagnosed as being caused by an excess of expenditures over income. Monetary contraction generated an excess demand for money that induced the increase in interest rates, which in turn caused a contraction in expenditures.

The hope was that by reducing aggregate demand, prices would fall at a speed and magnitude that would allow the real exchange rate to rise (in spite of the fact that the nominal rate was fixed) and recuperate the previous loss of competitiveness. This never occurred. Automatic adjustment proved to be very slow, and the magnitude of the recession, required to bring prices down, was too high to be sustainable, even in an authoritarian framework. In July 1982 the fixed exchange rate policy was abandoned, and, as these pages are written, pressures for a profound reversal of policies had increased, including higher tariffs, soft loans, active monetary policy, and increased government expenditures. The emerging picture was not too different from the Argentine experience after 1980.

4

Ideology and Institutional Reform in the Radical Conservative Experiment
The Chilean Case After 1973

THE previous chapter dealt with economic changes in the Chilean experiment with neoconservative economics. But the experiment in its more radical version also encompasses drastic, revolutionary changes in existing institutions, including labor legislation, social security reform, the way social services are provided, regional decentralization, and drafting a new constitution that modifies most institutions in the society.

It is not the objective of this book to study all these matters in detail, but an appropriate and thorough identification of what we have called the radical conservative experiment would be incomplete without some reference to these changes. We will concentrate here in one area of institutional changes, those comprised by the so-called "seven modernizations," which constitute the core of the radical conservative program in Chile in its mature stage, that is, after 1979.

An understanding of the real meaning of the seven modernizations as a program of institutional reform is not possible without a study of the ideology behind these reforms. Was this ideology present from the beginning of the experiment or did it gradually evolve from a narrow technocratic view of how to stabilize the economy toward a more global program of revolutionary changes in the sphere of the economy and society? We

91

will examine this question in the first section of this chapter. A second section will describe institutional reforms encompassed within the seven modernizations. This will serve as an illustration of the radical conservative ideology in practice.

The Process of Formulation of an Ideology

It is our hypothesis that the radical conservative ideology, although subjacent in restricted groups from the beginning, becomes the predominant ideology only after a long process of evolution that starts, in the economic sphere, from a basically technocratic view of how the economy should adjust in order to make the reduction of inflation and other disequilibria possible. It then evolves toward a more ambitious program of economic reform. We will attempt to describe this process of evolution, to end this section with an analysis of the resulting ideology that will provide the intellectual basis for the program of modernizations.

Initially, the orthodox economic program is presented as just a technically sound and neutral way of bringing the economy back to equilibrium. This is very much in the tradition of monetarism, as represented by the Chicago School. Economics as a positive science is capable of providing policymakers with a scientific answer to specific policy questions, according to this view. Since economic phenomena are regulated by a few basic economic laws, it is the task of the policymaker to derive from them those policy actions that are consistent with scientific laws governing economic relations. If this is the case, economic policies are technically sound.

When this theory is applied to economic stabilization, it means that optimal policies are those that tackle the problem of inflation at its origins. If a law of economics states that "in-

1. The expression is Milton Friedman's.

flation is always and everywhere a monetary phenomenon,"[1] it follows that the scientific way of dealing with the problem of inflation is by controlling money and the variables affecting its rate of expansion. In this sense, the initial monetarist stabilization program in Chile was nothing more than what was considered by the policymaker to be a technically sound way of restoring equilibrium in the economy.

But this technocratic vision prevalent at the beginning of the experiment had little to do with what was going on in the political sphere, where an authoritarian government had grabbed power by force and had sought to restore order by reversing previous political trends. After all, the military coup represented the culmination of a long process characterized by social and political disorder, accumulated inefficiencies in the economic sphere, and the pervading feeling among the traditional elites that power ebbs away from them in unpredictable directions. Before the coup, there was no clear ideology that acted as a cohesive force behind the various civilian and military groups in the opposition. There was only the slow gestation of a group of highly trained technocrats who observed events, particularly in the economy, and resented everything that was being done as counter to economic rationality and to a technically sound way of solving economic problems. The military reacted to political chaos that derived from an exacerbated social and political conflict. The traditional conservative elites sensed the possibility of mobilizing middle-class support for a drastic political change. But it was not clear at the time what type of change (restoration? revolution?) would be possible.

When the military took over, technocrats were called in to restore order in the economy. A stabilization program was put forth that represented a strictly technocratic solution to the problem of economic disequilibrium and extended inefficiencies. The military set for themselves the task of restoring order in social and political life by the use of force and political repression. The traditional conservative elites gave their support to the new government and waited for an opportunity to influence events.

It was not until a later stage that the ideological effort began. When the coalition was well established in power, the need was felt to provide a rationale for the changes in the power structure that were already taking place. In the economic sphere, the initial technocratic package encountered unexpected difficulties and restrictions. Results were not satisfactory, and policy failures were frequent. The way out of these difficulties was by proposing more radical changes in the economic structure so that expected "rational" behavior necessary for the success of the technocratic policies would be forthcoming. It was in this manner that objective conditions pushed simultaneously from the political and economic spheres in the direction of formulating a more global ideological and political project.

We will now illustrate the process of gestation of a global ideology from the perspective of economic policymaking. More specifically, we will discuss the way in which the initial technocratic orthodox stabilization package evolved toward a global economic paradigm useful not only to analyze economic problems but to illuminate the more general issues concerning the organization of society at a social, political, and even cultural level. The "stylized process" that we will describe corresponds closely with the Chilean experience although some of its traits may also be encountered in other experiences.[2]

At the beginning, the military felt the need to recuperate the economy from what they perceived as inefficient and politically motivated mishandling during the previous regime. The main

2. Useful reference material, complementary to my own elaboration, can be found in T. Moulian and P. Vergara, "Estado, ideología y políticas económicas en Chile 1973–1978," in *Colección Estudios CIEPLAN, No. 3, 1980.* Their excellent paper has influenced my thoughts on this topic.

credential of monetarists was their impeccable technical background: knowing how to do things in a scientific, nonpolitical way. The first task was to put the house in order. For this to be achieved, previous trends had to be reversed. If prices had been controlled, they were now set free. If the exchange rate had been pegged, a devaluation was in order. Of course, this made economic sense, given initial conditions, and was not seen as part of a strong ideological drive.

Once prices were right, or so it was believed, other technical tasks had to be performed, the main one being that of reducing the rate of inflation. Monetarism provided the answer to that: money supply should not expand as rapidly as it did, and, for this to happen, the fiscal deficit must be reduced. The solution, at a minimum nonideological level, was to reduce expenditures and increase tax revenues, but in the process—the argument may be put more strongly—which represented a first step in the direction of ideological escalation. Inflation was now attributed to the existence of too large a public sector. In the words of a finance minister: "Inflation . . . will continue decreasing as long as we are able to eradicate the main cause which is nothing other than the excessive size of the public sector."[3]

Hence, for inflation to be controlled, public employment must be reduced, public enterprises ought to be turned over to the private sector, and government should decrease its regulatory and developmental roles. In other words, a smaller public sector and a more significant private sector, which was part of the desired long-term political and structural change, was justified during this phase as a strictly technical question related to the containment of inflationary pressures.

Up to this point, the underlying economic ideology was not very different from that prevailing in conservative economic thinking in the United States, as the following shows:

3. Ministerio de Hacienda de Chile, *Exposición del Ministerio de Hacienda,* June 13, 1974.

What is occurring today is a concerted campaign to exploit popular discontent with inflation to reduce the relative size of the public sector and to reverse the income redistribution effected by government taxes and transfers. These objectives are legitimate political agenda, which deserve debate and decision on their merits. But they have nothing to do with inflation, and monetarist-conservatives (there is no logical necessity for this almost invariable combination) should be the first to point this out.[4]

In a second phase, the technical monetarist package escalated to a more drastic, intense application of orthodoxy. This phase occurred when, after several months of deregulation and destatization of economic activities, the results of the economic program were not only poor but did not show significant improvement as time went on. Monthly inflation rates were extremely high, recessionary signs were clearly visible, and no external resources flowed in. Either an external event, like a deterioration in the terms of trade, or poor domestic economic performance would trigger a change in the emphasis of the policies. In order to safeguard the integrity of the stabilization program, the process of adjustment had to accelerate: a more drastic reduction in public expenditures and employment was required, as well as a faster transfer of public assets to the private sector. The economy had to open up more rapidly to external trade as a way of checking domestic price increases through competition from imports. Thus, at this stage, poor economic performance partially disguised as the result of noncontrollable exogenous events was used to justify a deepening of policy measures that represented a more rapid and drastic reversion of previous trends: less government and more free markets.[5]

4. J. Tobin, "Stabilization Policy Ten Years After," *Brookings Papers on Economic Activity,* No. 1, 1980.
5. The "shock treatment" phase in Chile (1975–1976) corresponds closely with this description. See A. Foxley, "Stabilization Policies and Stagflation:

A third phase occurred when (and if) a relative success was achieved in reducing the rate of inflation and improving the balance of payments. At this time, some structural objectives as free trade, free private capital markets, and free flow of external financial resources were advocated per se, independent of the stabilization objectives. They were proposed as essential elements of a more efficient and dynamic process of economic growth in the long run. As a proof of their importance, they often carried a higher priority in policy decisions than the shorter-term stabilization objectives as such.

Policymakers were willing to pay a price in terms of a slower reduction in the rate of inflation or of a longer recession, provided the momentum was maintained in the direction of deeper long-term transformation of the economic structure. There were instances in which decisions in the field of tariff reductions, interest rates, international capital flows deregulation, and institutional changes in financial institutions were bound to produce negative effects in short-term stabilization goals and were certainly not optimal from a purely technical point of view in order to stabilize the economy. But they were now justified as a function of required structural changes for better long-term performance.[6]

Up until now the main objective of the policies still consisted of reversing previous trends. The implicit, desired institutional scheme corresponded very much to that of a mixed economy, with an enhanced role for the market. It was not until later, when the economy was showing strong signs of recuperation, that a more ambitious program of economic transforma-

The Cases of Brazil and Chile," in A. Foxley and L. Whitehead, eds., *Economic Stabilization in Latin America: Political Dimensions* (Pergamon, 1980). A similar, although milder version was attempted in Argentina in 1977 and 1978. See R. Frenkel, "La apertura financiera externa: El caso argentino," paper presented to the Conference on International Financial Markets and Their Impact on Latin America, CIEPLAN (mimeo), Santiago, March 1981.

6. Moulian and Vergara; "Estado, ideología y políticas económicas."

tion began to be voiced. This occurred when the political con-solidation of the regime had progressed to the point that political action could be programed as part of a long-term strategy, not only as a reaction to internal and external political crisis and events.

At this point the more enlightened of technocrats, intellec-tuals, and the modern segment of the business community began to articulate a more coherent, doctrinaire view of the "subsidiary role of the state" and what it implies in terms of privatization. Why should there be limits to privatization of public enterprises? Why would it be necessary for copper or steel production, or the railroads, port administration, electric-ity, and oil production and distribution be public sector activi-ties? What sound economic argument is there behind the mili-tary's view of some enterprises being "strategical" and the reason for their remaining in the public sector?

Consistent with this view, new policies were undertaken. The last vestiges of land reform were eliminated. Land reform legislation was abolished, as well as all zoning regulations, thus limiting the use of agricultural and urban land. New transfers of property away from peasants occurred. Urban land specula-tion became a highly profitable activity. The withdrawal of the state from the provision of health, education, and social secu-rity benefits and its consequent privatization was proposed. Ambitious new institutional arrangements for the private pro-vision of these services were conceived and began to be imple-mented. The government felt itself immersed now in a process of historical transformation identified as the seven moderni-zations.

Finally, the experiment reached a stage of maturity. It was now recognized that the government's objective was nothing less than a "revolución en el terreno de la economía" and in-deed a revolution that would permeate all of society. There were main tasks during this phase: one was to find a way of reabsorbing the excluded sectors, mainly labor, into the new structures. How to turn the lion into a cat, without compromising the firm march toward the modernizations was the challenge. New labor legislation and a complete transformation of the social security system had to perform that function by defining new rules of the game under which collective bargaining and organized labor's presence was not threatening anymore.

The other critical task was to solve the basic contradiction in the model: how can economic freedom be made consistent with political authoritarianism? How is it possible to conceive of a relationship between the new economic structures and a new political and institutional system that preserves the nature of the state and the social relations of production, even when there is a regime change? Once again, the solution to this problem was to be provided by technocrats in a scientific way. The methodology was to be borrowed from economic science, whose inner logic had proved to be, in the view of regime supporters, such a powerful instrument in diagnosing the ills and shaping rational and efficient solutions in the sphere of the economy. It now would be used for a grander design: shaping the new political and legal institutions that would sustain a new economy and a new society. Economics was now hailed as a "superscience."[7]

How can the principles of economics be used in the analysis of sociopolitical problems? The neoconservative argument, in its Latin American version, is as follows. Economics as a science is based on the assumption of individual rationality. Every individual seeks to maximize his own satisfaction (preferences), and the market is shown to be the most efficient instrument in order to achieve this objective. The market solution is optimal

7. The expression is Gordon Tullock's at a public conference sponsored by the Centro de Estudios Públicos, idelogical think-tank of neoconservatives in Chile; see *Ercilla* (Santiago), Dec. 24, 1980.

for everybody concerned. On the other hand, preferences as expressed through the market are independent of any form of coercion, particularly that arising from political institutions.[8] Political institutions are believed to be used by individuals to obtain gains from others through some form of coercion.[9] Only the market is free from the contaminating force of politics. This is the reason for a free market as the foundation on which all individual freedoms are based.

Given the superiority of market rationality, it is only natural for neoconservatives to apply the same principles in order to seek "rational" decisions elsewhere in the social and political system. If public officials and bureaucrats follow the same self-maximizing objectives in public institutions as they would as individuals, the institutions' desired general objectives get distorted. The way to minimize distortions is to reduce the role of political institutions as much as possible and let most decisions be made where real freedom of choice exists, and this is none other than the market.[10]

The political consequence of the previous reasoning is that the state should withdraw as much as possible from decision making in society and that a process of decentralization and privatization of decision making should accompany it. By this

8. The following quotation from Fontaine reveals the influence of Milton Friedman on neoconservative intellectuals in Latin America: "The market provides economic freedom, and since preferences expressed in the market are independent of political authority and indeed of other forms of coercion as well, [it is the market] that sustains individual freedom in a broader sense than merely a strictly economic sense, according to Milton Friedman"; see A. Fontaine, "Más allá del Leviatan," *Estudios Públicos,* No. 1, Centro de Estudios Públicos, Santiago, Dec. 1980.

9. "Political institutions offer the opportunity to acquire a control over resources by socially nonproductive methods"—Karl Brunner "Reflexiones sobre la economía política del gobierno," *Estudios Públicos,* No. 1, Centro de Estudios Públicos, Santiago, 1980.

10. This argument is borrowed by Latin American neoconservatives from the "public choice" approach in the United States as developed by J. Buchanan, G. Tullock, and others.

means, political power, and the coercion that would derive from it, dissolves itself in individual decision making under market-type situations. This is very much at the core of neoconservative thinking.

But how are decisions going to be made in such a decentralized setting when nonmarketable goods such as a new law or constitution must be voted upon? Democratic electoral processes have been shown to be seriously handicapped. People vote with imperfect knowledge. Decisions between alternatives can be shown to depend on the number of alternatives presented, on the order in which they are presented, and several other distorting factors. Thus, getting as close to a unanimity rule as possible is desirable as a way to check the degree of distortion and to avoid a wrong reading of revealed preferences.[11]

The paradigm so far seems to be a logical extension of free market principles. Economic freedom achieved through the market is extended to other decisions by reducing the role of political institutions (like the executive and legislative branches) and taking decisions back to the individual. This is risky, given biases in voting mechanisms, but preferable to discretionary, coercive political power.

What if not only voting processes are imperfect but, in addition, individuals are not rational in the ways that market allocation requires? What if they prefer economic security instead of maximizing their preferences through risky market interaction? This is all possible, according to this view, when individuals have been submitted for a long period to the influence of an all-too-powerful, benevolent government that takes care of their basic needs. If socialism has crept into the minds of people, so the argument goes, rational behavior cannot be ex-

11. J. Buchanan, "De las preferencias privadas a una filosofía del sector público," *Estudios Públicos*, No. 1, Centro de Estudios Públicos, Santiago, 1980.

pected—at least not until the superiority of the new, free market principles has been widely demonstrated.[12] A rationale has now been provided for not allowing democratic decision mechanisms to operate. This role may be better fulfilled, so the ideologues would say, by an enlightened central authority that can perceive what the rational (scientific) solutions are and is thus able to guide people to social optimality. Authority must be strong and vigilant, given the fragility of market mechanisms, when faced with less than rational public opinion.[13]

What we have broadly described is the ideological evolution of monetarism and neoconservative ideas closely following one case that is usually considered by monetarist advocates as a successful one.[14] As we see the argument develop, monetarism evolves from simple, short-term technical prescriptions to stabilize the economy, toward a radical view of a free market economy and society, organized around the principles of economic freedom and—one would think as a logical counterpart—political liberalism. But here the basic ideology is twisted to fit political convenience: although political freedom may be desirable, it cannot be achieved as long as irrational behavior persists, lest the advance toward free markets is compromised.

A rationale has finally been provided to solve the basic contradiction in the long-term view of the economy as it relates to the social and political system: economic freedom must coexist with authoritarian government for the model to be viable, at least dur-

12. The process is a long one. In the words of an influential supporter of the regime: "From [new] values to a sense of personal responsibility, there is a vast process of reeducation that has to be faced. Once bad habits created in more than forty years of decadence are eradicated, only then will the country recuperate its vitality"—Pedro Ibañez, *Qué Pasa* (Santiago), Jan. 3, 1980.

13. The following illustrates the point: "Very often decentralization will require the exercise of a vigorous authority that will prevail over the obstacles facing the freedom of the market"—Fontaine, "Más allá del Leviatan."

14. We refer to the evolution of official monetarist-conservative thinking in the Chilean case.

ing the (long) process when people learn and educate themselves in the advantage of free markets and small government.

Institutional Changes and Ideology: The Seven Modernizations

Institutional developments in Chile since the military coup in 1973 reflect well the process of ideological escalation described in the previous section. Particularly illuminating is the institutional evolution in the later stages, beginning in mid-1979. We will describe in this section those institutional changes that affected most directly the way the economy operated in the mature period of the experiment. These were the so-called seven modernizations. These changes represented good examples of the attempt to solve in practice the contradictions between the free market, decentralized economic model and the highly centralized and authoritarian political model, referred to in the previous section.

In September 1979, General Pinochet announced that "having reached some of the goals of national reconstruction, the government would now become a government of national modernization."[15] This was described by a labor minister as a "crucial stage in this truly silent revolution that is taking place in Chile."[16] The modernizations referred to drastic changes in seven areas: labor policy, social security, education, health, regional decentralization, agriculture, and justice. The objective of the modernizations was described as "the promotion of integral development of the country, of a dominating presence of rationality, and a perfected freedom for men in their more immediate preoccupations."[17]

15. *El Mercurio* (Santiago), Sept. 12, 1979.
16. J. Piñera, *Qué Pasa*, Dec. 27, 1979.
17. *El Mercurio*, Sept. 16, 1979.

The intended direction of economic reforms were then to decentralize public institutions, leave as many of these activities as possible to the private sector, let market decision making operate, and, in a general way, guarantee freedom of choice to individuals concerning the provision and access to basic social services.[18] At a more political level, it was wished that "each worker feels that the way things go with the functioning of the [new] economy will go for him also."[19] Of the seven modernizations, perhaps the labor and social security reforms reflected most closely these objectives, particularly the need to reincorporate the workers as active participants, committed to the goals of the new economic model. We will refer mostly to these two and then only briefly indicate the general characteristic of the other programs of modernization in the social sectors.

The labor reform ("Plan Laboral") was put into effect in June 1979 and represented an attempt to solve the problem of exclusion of labor organizations from collective bargaining or any other forms of economic participation that had been in effect since after the military coup in 1973.[20] On the positive side, the new labor legislation guaranteed a floor for wage increases, indexing wages to past inflation. On the other hand, the new legislation authorized the constitution of labor unions by enterprise under the principle of free affiliation. It sufficed that if 10% of the workers in an enterprise decided to form a union, then they could proceed and negotiate separately with management. In firms with less than twenty-five workers, eight workers or more could form a union. Workers who were not union members could also negotiate with the firm, subject to the same conditions as unions. Labor federations or any association of

18. Ibid.
19. *Qué Pasa*, Dec. 27, 1979.
20. See, J. Piñera, in *Qué Pasa*, July 11, 1979. For critical evaluations, see J. Ruiz-Tagle, "El Nuevo Plan Laboral," *Mensaje*, No. 281, Aug. 1979; and VECTOR (Center of Socioeconomic Studies), *Informe de Coyuntura* (Santiago), July 1980.

several unions was not allowed to participate in collective bargaining. Workers located in services and the public sector were also excluded from collective bargaining.

The right to strike was guaranteed, but subject to severe limitations. The maximum period allowed for a strike was sixty days, after which the workers were automatically fired. After thirty days, any union member could go back to work without sanctions. As few as 10% of the workers could censor labor negotiators at any time. The firm could hire temporary workers to substitute for strikers the moment the strike began. And firms also had the right to a lockout.

As a result of the legislation, worker organizations proliferated, many within a single firm, each bargaining separately. The procedure regulating strikes debilitated workers' bargaining position as days went by since after sixty days, if there was no agreement, either conditions previous to the negotiation were accepted or the workers were fired.

What was sought with this legislation was that "free" unions took part in collective bargaining in a decentralized manner that was not threatening to the rationality of the economic model. This meant that it did not disrupt production except in a very localized and temporary fashion. And by atomizing the labor movement, it sought to prevent the regaining of political (or at least counterbalancing) power that union organizations long had had in Chile. Free markets, decentralization, and political immobilization and control were all achieved at once.

Social security reform pursued similar goals. The social security system was changed from a pay-as-you-go basis to an individual savings scheme.[21] Workers' social security contributions were mandatory, but they did not go to decentralized public institutions but to private companies. Workers could freely choose with which institution they affiliated. The private

21. This analysis is based on J. P. Arellano, "Elementos para el análisis de la reforma previsional," CIEPLAN (mimeo), Santiago, June 1981.

institutions that administered social security funds performed the function of investing workers' contributions in the capital market. For this, they got a commission and service charge. The rate of return obtained by an individual worker on his social security savings depended on the particular company's success in investing in highly profitable investment instruments. A minimum rate of return was guaranteed by law, but this minimum was variable and dependent on the average profitability in the financial sector.

In a country with permanent and high inflation and a generally unstable economy, rates of return in financial investments may vary over a wide range from negative to positive rates. But whatever the variability, once the workers affiliate with the new private institutions that administer their retirement funds, they soon realize that their "fate" is closely related to that of the companies where their funds are invested. The worker will tend to become an indirect partner, interested in the success of the financial sector and the firms where social security funds are invested. The threatening behavior of workers vis-à-vis the free market, capitalist system is defused.

Another practical consequence of the scheme is that by transferring social security funds from the public to the private sector, what is transferred is the command over a huge volume of long-term investment resources, which have been estimated as 20% of GDP, accumulated over a ten-year period.[22] Who got command over these resources? Empirical evidence shows that after two months of implementation of the scheme, the two largest conglomerates ("grupos económicos") acquired control of 75% of the market.[23]

Why did this concentration take place? Uncertain economic conditions, unstable financial markets, cyclical economic behavior, and significant inflation made workers unsure about what a rational decision concerning affiliation in the

22. Ibid.   23. *El Mercurio,* July 15, 1981.

new system would be. Rather than calculating expected rates of return in various alternatives, it seemed that a presumed higher security attached to investing in the largest groups would protect against the risk of bankruptcies, default, or unwise financial decisions that tended to happen frequently in unstable economic environments. Hence, most workers freely chose to strengthen the most powerful economic groups by putting their social security contributions there. Workers became unsuspecting agents reinforcing the pattern of asset concentration that characterized the radical conservative experiment.

Other effects of the change in the social security scheme pointed in the same direction, although they originated in the problems of the transition from the old to the new system rather than from a necessary characteristic of the private scheme as such. During the transition, older workers remained affiliated to the public social security institutions, but other workers transferred to the new system. What this means is that the public sector had to pay benefits to older workers without receiving contributions from younger, more productive workers. It was estimated that the public sector would cease to receive contributions equivalent to 5% of GDP annually, and yet it had to pay retirement pensions not too different from the historical trend, at least in the transition years.[24]

The resulting larger deficit would force the government to reduce expenditures more or to transfer assets to the private sector. More privatization would occur as a result. And if previous patterns remained, this would most probably reinforce the trend toward asset concentration within the private sector. Free markets, privatization, and decentralization in social security were not necessarily equivalent to a more equal distribution of income, assets, and power emerging from the new scheme.

Modernization in the social sectors (education, health, re-

24. Arellano, "Elementos para el análisis."

gional decentralization, etc.) followed similar principles of transferring resources to the private sector or municipalities and away from the central government. These reforms also sought to develop a private market for educational, health, housing, and nutrition services, where individuals should be able to buy the best services available in a competitive environment. The government only guaranteed the provision of free minimum services to the very poor.[25]

The allocation of public funds for these purposes would be highly centralized, and public institutions distributing them at the local level would be directly dependent on the president, the highest political authority and holder of vast powers in the authoritarian regime.[26] Economic decentralization and political centralization of decisions would go hand in hand.

A better understanding of this strange blend of market liberalism and political authoritarian centralization is obtained when attention is paid to changes in the political institutions that were taking place more or less simultaneously with the seven modernizations. In September 1980 a new constitution was enforced; its objective was to define the nature of the political institutions that emerged from the revolutionary process of transformation, to which we have referred in this and previous chapters. The constitution had the peculiar feature that it would not be fully applicable until nine years after it was approved. Meanwhile, "transitory" emergency regulations would prevail.[27]

25. See *El Mercurio,* Sept. 16, 1981; T. Valdivia, "El proyecto educacional del gobierno," *Mensaje,* No. 278, May 1979; J. Ruiz-Tagle, "La nueva política de salud," *Mensaje,* No. 280, July 1979; A. Goic, "Salud en Chile: El problema de fondo," *Mensaje,* No. 282, Sept. 1979; José F. Mesa, "El modelo actual y la experiencia agraria," *Mensaje,* No. 283, Oct. 1979.

26. P. Vergara, "Las transformaciones del Estado chileno bajo el régimen militar," *Colección Estudios CIEPLAN,* No. 5, 1981.

27. See *Qué Pasa,* March 12, 1981; *Ercilla* (Santiago), March 4, 1981; *ASPI* (magazine), March 10, 1981; *Mensaje,* Nos. 292 and 298, Sept. 1980 and May 1981, respectively.

Under the new constitution a transition period of seventeen years (after the constitution was approved) was defined. Only after this period presidents would be freely elected as they are in Western democracies. Meanwhile, the powers of the presidency were reinforced. During the first eight years, no parliament or political parties were allowed. The president could at any time, without consulting any institutional body or individual, declare a state of emergency, during which individuals' rights could be curtailed or suppressed. Habeas corpus had no legal validity during the emergency.[28]

As a more permanent feature, the armed forces were given the role of guarantors of the "institutional order." Through a National Security Council they could make their views known to any political body or institution, and they could request any information they desired.[29]

At the same time that political participation and free democratic decisions were suppressed for a long transition period, "economic freedom" was guaranteed. In fact, as explained in the section on ideology, the former was seen as unavoidable in order to ensure the latter during the transition phase.

28. M. Montealegre, "Una constitución encerrada en el pasado," *Mensaje*, No. 293, Oct. 1980.
29. See *Qué Pasa*, March 12, 1981.

PART TWO

The Neoconservative Economic Stabilization Policies

5

Neoconservative Policies
and Economic Stabilization

WE have so far looked at neoconservative economics in its Latin American practice from a broad perspective, including a detailed appraisal of its more radical version, the Chilean case. We will devote the next chapters to an evaluation of neoconservative policies in their narrower objective of achieving economic stabilization.

Our main interest in the first section of this chapter will be to explore technically and suggest possible explanations for the economics in its Latin American practice from a broad perspective economic stabilization policies in Latin America. We will tackle the question: Are we dealing with a unique, unchanged theoretical framework or with an evolving one? We must stress the tentative nature of the explanations. In fact, at a minimum level, they might even be considered a "reasonable working hypothesis" concerning the phenomena with which we will be dealing. A more definitive formulation must await a better data base and more empirical testing than was available or possible to the author.

In the second section we will describe stylized results for the stabilization programs in Latin America, results useful for providing the right focus on the next two chapters. In Chapter 6 we will explore the economics of economic stabilization from the point of view of theory and general empirical evidence, and in Chapter 7 we will examine the monetarist-conservative stabilization policies by looking at each of the main policy instruments. We will attempt to assess the likely impact that each has had on the stabilization goals.

The Evolution from Conventional to Open Economy Monetarism

Monetarist stabilization policies in countries like Chile, Argentina, and Uruguay in the second half of the seventies represented a clear, simple, if somewhat rigid set of measures whose principal virtue was its coherence with respect to a powerful and robust body of theory. This corresponded to monetarism as popularized by Milton Friedman and other Chicago School economists. Inflation was "always and everywhere a monetary phenomenon," and its cure must be found in the contraction of money supply, in the elimination of the fiscal deficit, and in setting the "prices right," including currency devaluation when needed. As has been argued before, this was the basic policy framework behind Latin American monetarism in the 1970s.

However, when the policies are evaluated more carefully, we find at least two other theoretical frameworks. One of these represents a change in emphasis to cost pressures and inflationary expectations as sources of inflation. It is claimed that built-in indexing is at least partly responsible for the perpetuation of inflation. Policies then shift toward the gradual deindexation of critical prices: the exchange rate, public utility rates, and wages. The main effort of the government is put in enforcing rigid deindexation rules and in trying to increase the credibility of the gradual disinflationary targets. Monetary contraction continues to play a role but not the central one. Indeed, the "new" stabilization theory reflects to a large extent the frustrations of policymakers in trying unsuccessfully to enforce strict monetarism. We shall illustrate this later with the Argentine case.

A third theoretical framework appears when the economy has advanced to deregulating trade and external financial flows. In the open economy, money supply is an endogenously determined variable. Why is money supply endogenous? The two main components of the monetary base are loans to the national treasury and changes in reserves. Of these, the first one is irrelevant once the fiscal deficit has been brought under control. The change in international reserves, on the other hand, is an endogenous variable. It depends on the size of the trade deficit and on external capital flows, which are regulated by the difference between international and domestic interest rates, adjusted by expected devaluation of domestic currency. At the same time, if the economy is fully open and all goods are tradable internationally, the domestic price level is just a function of international prices and the exchange rate.

This new theoretical framework, referred to as the monetary approach to the balance of payments, has replaced the more conventional form of monetarism. This new framework became a useful device to justify a marked change in the approach to stabilization. In the Latin American experience, this change occurred in the middle of the stabilization effort, 1978 in Argentina and 1979 in Chile. Where previously the control of money supply was the critical variable, now it was irrelevant; fixed exchange rates replaced the crawling peg as the optimal exchange rate policy; reserve accumulation was not considered a problem for monetary policy; quite the contrary, it allowed for a smooth adjustment of domestic inflation rates to external inflation.

How was this policy reversal justified within the new theoretical framework? According to the new paradigm, once we are dealing with an open economy, the process of economic adjustment is substantially modified. Suppose that, for a given exchange rate, the monetary authority decides to reduce domestic credit expansion. This action, essential in the conventional monetarist approach for the closed economy, will not be effective now. To be sure, credit restriction will have a contractionary effect on money supply, but the adjustment of the economy to monetary contraction will be different. Given a certain demand for real cash balances reduction in money supply will result in an excess demand for money. Two effects will follow. The first is a rise in domestic interest rates that will attract an inflow of foreign capital. This will increase net reserves and expand money supply, partly compensating for the previous reduction. A second effect will occur because the public, in the face of scarce money, will try to replenish its desired level of cash balances by withdrawing money from transactions. This will make expenditures and income fall. The contraction in monetary income will in turn affect imports. A lower demand for imports will reduce the trade deficit, also increasing net reserves and thus having an additional expansionary effect in money supply. The mechanism will operate automatically until the original equilibrium is restored.

This policy action was futile. Money supply adjusted automatically to the original rate of expansion. Domestic prices did not go down (or the rate of increase did not go down). In fact, the theory predicts that domestic prices will not grow faster than external prices except for movements in the exchange rate. The process of adjustment may be slow if there remain internal sources of money creation like a significant public sector deficit. But once this has been eliminated, the internal rate of inflation should converge to the international rate unless devaluations occur. Since policymakers favor automatic adjustment in the economy at this stage and an "equilibrium" rate of inflation equal to external inflation, a strong preference develops for a fixed exchange rate policy.

The way these various theoretical approaches influenced policy were appreciated when we described the phases of Chilean stabilization policies in an earlier chapter. Another interesting one is that of Argentina after 1976 under the military government of General Videla. The Argentinian case provides a particularly clear example of practical monetarism in search of a theory.[1] The initial focus of the Argentinian policy in early 1976 consisted of drastically devaluating the peso, reducing real wages and the government deficit, deregulating prices, and eliminating subsidies and nontariff restrictions to trade. Surprisingly, in spite of verbal support for an active monetary policy, money supply expanded *pari passu* with prices, partly the result of a surplus in the balance of payments that developed within a few months of implementation of the new policies.

By late 1976 prices were increasing at a monthly rate of between 8% and 14%. After a brief, unsuccessful experiment with price control, the government decided in June 1977 to apply monetary contraction in a more consistent manner. This policy was undertaken simultaneously with the elimination of price controls and with a financial reform that liberalized credit markets, freeing up the interest rate.

Monetary contraction did not last very long. In fact, credit restrictions accompanied by deregulation of interest rates led to a big upsurge in nominal interest rates. Monthly rates doubled from 6% in June to 13% in December. This generated two simultaneous effects: on the one hand, higher prices and a slowdown in industrial production; on the other, a rapid increase in capital inflows. This resulted in an unprogramed expansion in money supply.

Financial liberalization, which was a key component of the policy package, was seriously complicating monetary management. An indication is given by the fact that by the end of 1977, two-thirds of high-powered money originated in accumulation of reserves. After a few months of trying to regulate simultaneously the inflow of capital and the expansion of domestic credit, the effort was abandoned in May 1978.

At this point a new theoretical approach provided a ration-

1. A complete description of the various phases of economic policy in Argentina is found in R. Frenkel, "Inflación y política anti-inflacionaria Argentina 1975–1978," CEDES (mimeo), Buenos Aires, 1980.

ale for a very different set of policies. It was thought that excess demand could not be responsible for the persistently high inflation, currently around 10% a month, since recessionary signs were all too evident across the industrial sector. Industrial output in 1978 was 8% below 1977 levels. The emphasis shifted to curbing cost pressures and inflationary expectations. Instead of letting indexation mechanisms validate expected inflation, prices would be readjusted only a fraction of expected inflation. Deindexation was the key to the new policies.

But by the end of 1978, the economy was more open. Nontariff restrictions had been eliminated, and tariffs were gradually being reduced. Deindexation of the exchange rate implied a substantial appreciation of the peso. This plus tariff reductions were rapidly exposing the sheltered industrial sector to competition from imports. Remaining restrictions on capital inflows were eliminated. Once this was done, money became an endogenous variable. Monetary policy was passive. Except for preannounced values for the exchange rate and public utility rates, other variables in the system would adjust by the automatic mechanisms suggested by the monetary approach to the balance of payments: by free capital flows and by what was thought to be an inevitable trend toward interest rate and inflation rate equalization between the domestic and the international economy. Open economy monetarism became the accepted and preferred approach to economic stabilization. Somewhat similar phases were observed in the evolution of policies in the Chilean case although policy consistency tended to be higher, and inconsistencies and changes were of minor importance when compared with post-1976 Argentina. The several phases that can be distinguished in the Chilean case were described in Chapter 3 and will not be repeated here.

In sum, orthodox stabilization programs in Latin America in the 1970s and 1980s broadly represented the evolution of monetarist ideas. The old monetarism for the closed economy that had been in vogue in Latin America in the late 1950s, as well as during the first phase of the more recent stabilization policies, gradually gave way to open economy monetarism with its emphasis on the automaticity of the adjustment process. The transition from the old to the new approach was not an easy one. It required frequent adjustments. Mistakes were made, and policy actions did not often correspond to what was needed, as will be suggested by the more theoretical exploration of these issues in the next two chapters.

Policy Performance

As a way of providing a focus on the theoretical discussion of the issues around the monetarist stabilization approach in its Latin American practice that will follow in the next two chapters, we will now describe some macroeconomic results of several countries' experiences: Chile after 1973, Argentina after 1976, Uruguay from 1974, and Brazil in the period 1964–1967. Obviously the policies undertaken by these various governments have some similarities and several differences. They all share a monetarist origin irrespective of their different degrees of incorporation of nonorthodox elements in the policy package. Of the cases covered, Chile is by far the more orthodox, with Brazil at the other extreme.

A description of the policies, from which it is easy to infer both common elements and differences, can be found elsewhere.[2] We will summarize here some aggregate results. Figures for GDP, rates of inflation, wages and salaries, and the distribution of income or consumption for households are

2. See A. Ferrer, "El retorno del liberalismo: Reflexiones sobre la política económica vigente en la Argentina," *Desarrollo Económico* 18(72) (Jan. 1979); A. Canitrot and R. Frenkel, "Estabilización y largo plazo: La experiencia argentina 1976–1979," CEDES (mimeo), Buenos Aires, June 1979; and for the Chilean case, see Chapter 3 in this book. For the case of Uruguay, see "Un nuevo ensayo de reajuste económico: Uruguay 1974–79," CINVE, Montevideo, Dec. 1980.

TABLE 25

Variation in GDP and Consumer Prices:
Argentina, Brazil, Chile, and Uruguay
(annual growth rates)

	ARGENTINA			BRAZIL	
Year	GDP (1)	Consumer Prices (2)	Year	GDP (3)	Consumer Prices (4)
1974	6.1	40.1	1962	5.2	51.3
1975	−0.9	334.9	1963	1.5	81.3
1976	−1.7	347.5	1964	2.9	91.9
1977	4.9	160.4	1965	2.7	34.5
1978	−3.4	169.9	1966	3.8	38.8
1979	8.5	139.7	1967	4.8	24.3

	CHILE			URUGUAY	
Year	GDP (5)	Consumer Prices (6)	Year	GDP (7)	Consumer Prices (8)
1973	−1.1	605.9	1973	0.8	77.5
1974	4.2	369.2	1974	3.1	107.3
1975	−16.6	343.3	1975	4.4	66.8
1976	5.0	197.9	1976	2.6	39.9
1977	8.6	84.2	1977	3.4	57.3
1978	6.0	37.2	1978	3.9	46.0
1979	8.5	38.9	1979	8.4	83.1

Sources:
(1) Central Bank of Chile, *Memoria Anual.*
(2) CEPAL, *Estudio Económico de América Latina.*
(3) *Coyuntura Económica,* Nov. 1972 and July 1977.
(4) H. Lemgruber, *Inflation in Brazil* (Brookings Institution, 1977).

(5) ODEPLAN, *Cuentas Nacionales de Chile.*
(6) INE; and *Comentarios sobre la situación económica,* Department of Economics, University of Chile, 1978.
(7) Central Bank of Chile, *Indicadores Económico-Financieros.*
(8) Ibid.

TABLE 26

Unemployment Rates:
Buenos Aires, Montevideo, and Santiago
(percentages)

Year	Buenos Aires (1)	Montevideo (2)	Santiago (3)
1972	6.6	7.7	3.8
1973	5.4	8.9	4.6
1974	3.4	8.1	9.6
1975	3.7	—	16.3
1976	4.5	12.8	16.7
1977	3.0	11.8	13.2
1978	2.8	10.1	14.0
1979	2.0	—	13.6

Sources:
(1) PREALC, *Archivo de datos ocupacionales sobre América Latina y el Caribe,* 1979.

(2) Direc. Estadísticas, *Encuesta de Hogares.*
(3) Department of Economics, University of Chile, *Ocupación y desocupación.*

given in Tables 25, 26, 27, and 28. Stylized results suggest the following:

1. A resilience of the inflation rate despite sustained stabilization efforts: in three of the four cases considered, it takes between four and five years to bring the inflation rate to a level around 40% a year; and in the Argentinian case, after four years it was still around 150%.[3]

2. The coexistence of high inflation with recession during an equivalently long period (notice that in two of the four

3. Grouping all cases together is not totally fair, given the differences in the initial conditions—inflation in Brazil and Uruguay was about 90%, vis-à-vis more than 300% in Argentina and Chile.

TABLE 27 Real Wages Index: Argentina, Brazil, Chile, and Uruguay

ARGENTINA (1973 = 100)

Year	Average Wages Public Sector (1)	Average Wages Industry (2)	Average Salaries Industry (3)	Basic Wages Industry (4)	Basic Wages Agriculture (5)
1973	100.0	100.0	100.0	100.0	100.0
1974	110.0	114.0	116.0	103.8	114.7
1975	85.0	105.0	109.0	101.7	106.4
1976	58.0	72.0	78.0	58.5	58.9
1977	42.0		89.0	52.9	53.6

BRAZIL (1961 = 100)

Year	Median Wages Industry (Rio) (6)	Wages Rural Sector (S.P.) (7)	Minimum Wage (Rio) (8)
1961	100.0	100.0	100.0
1962	93.2	99.4	83.5
1963	89.6	92.2	77.4
1964		102.1	77.4
1965	85.4	116.7	71.3
1966	83.1	108.2	66.1
1967	86.5	117.6	63.5

CHILE (1970 = 100)

Year	Average Wages (9)	Average Salaries (10)
1973		
1974	65.8	64.9
1975	61.1	65.1
1976	65.0	65.0
1977	71.0	72.5
1978	76.0	76.4

URUGUAY (1970 = 100)

Year	Average Wages Industry (11)	Average Wages Agriculture (12)
1973	84.0	81.2
1974	83.5	87.8
1975	75.7	86.0
1976	68.5	90.2
1977	58.8	70.4

cases—Argentina and Chile—GDP per capita actually fell in real terms).

3. Unemployment went up sharply in at least two of the four cases, the extreme case being Chile where the rate of unemployment even went up between three and four times the historical rates.

4. Wages fell between 20% and 40% in real terms in all four cases.

5. The family income distribution, when available, showed a deterioration in the income share of the poorer and a significant gain for the higher quintile.

Some of these results were the consequence of a deliberate policy, the best example being the fall in real wages. Wage repression was a basic element in the orthodox policy package. Other results, like the prolonged period of high inflation and high unemployment, were not expected at all.[4] And yet these

4. The following quotation from P. Baraona, who was to become minister of economics in the Pinochet government, is illustrative. In October 1973 he declared: "Before a year, we will have a zero rate of inflation"; see *El Mercurio* (Santiago), Oct. 17, 1973.

Sources (Table 27):

(1) A. Canitrot and R. Frenkel, "Estabilización y largo plazo: La experiencia argentina 1976–1979," CEDES (mimeo), Buenos Aires, June 1979.

(2) Ibid.

(3) Ibid.

(4) PREALC, *Asalariados de bajos ingresos y salarios mínimos en América Latina,* 1979.

(5) Ibid.

(6) E. Bacha, "Economic Growth, Rural and Urban Wages: The Case of Brazil," Catholic University of Rio de Janeiro (mimeo), March 1979.

(7) E. Bacha and L. Taylor, "Brazilian Income Distribution in the 1960s: 'Facts,' Model Results, and the Controversy," *Journal of Development Studies* 14 (3) (April 1978).

(8) Bacha, "Economic Growth."

(9) Bacha and Taylor, "Brazilian Income Distribution."

(10) INE.

(11) PREALC, *Asalariados de bajos ingresos.*

(12) Ibid.

TABLE 28

Income Distribution
in Brazil and
Uruguay (Montevideo)
and Consumption
Distribution
in Chile (Santiago)
by Household Quintiles
(percentages)

BRAZIL		
Quintiles	1960 (1)	1970 (2)
I	3.49	3.16
II	8.07	6.85
III	13.81	10.81
IV	20.26	16.94
V	54.35	62.24

CHILE (Santiago)		
Quintiles	1969 (3)	1978 (4)
I	7.6	5.2
II	11.8	9.3
III	15.6	13.6
IV	20.5	20.9
V	44.5	51.0

Sources:
(1) and (2) E. Bacha and L. Taylor, "Brazilian Income Distribution in the 1960s: 'Facts,' Model Results, and the Controversy," *Journal of Development Studies* 14(3) (April 1978).
(3) and (4) INE, *Encuesta de Presupuestos Familiares.*
(5) and (6) J. Bensión and A. Canmant, *Política económica y distribución del ingreso en Uruguay 1970–1976,* Montevideo, 1979.

URUGUAY (Montevideo)		
Quintiles	1973 (5)	1976 (6)
I	6.53	5.52
II	11.34	10.21
III	15.94	15.06
IV	22.65	22.49
V	43.54	46.72

results are very important in explaining the process of income concentration that accompanied these experiences. In the next two chapters we will explore the reasons for a policy outcome that seems uniformly to be characterized by stagflation, defined here as the coexistence of high inflation and sustained recession, and by a worsening in the distribution of income.

6

The Economics
of Stabilization
Policies and
Stagflation

CHAPTER 5 dealt with the evolution of
neoconservative stabilization policies from conventional to
open economy monetarism. It also gave some comparative aggregate results of the policies in several countries. From these
results we inferred some common elements. One of these was
that the stabilization policies led to a period characterized by
high inflation and recession that was longer than expected by
policymakers. This we called the stagflationary effects of the
policies, using a broad definition of stagflation: the persistence
of high inflation and recession. In turn, recessions will often
result in higher unemployment. If not, there will be an increase
in underemployment. That is why stagflation is often also identified with situations of high inflation and high unemployment.[1]

In this chapter and the next we will try to understand what
generated that kind of result by exploring the relationship between stabilization policies and stagflation. In the first section
we will summarize the main hypotheses, then elaborate on
them in the following two sections. Next, we will examine em-

1. For useful surveys on these topics, see R. J. Gordon, "Recent Development in the Theory of Inflation and Unemployment," in E. Lundberg, ed., *Inflation Theory and Antiinflation Policy* (Westview Press, 1977); and D. Laidler
and J. Parkin, "Inflation: A Survey," *Economic Journal,* 1975.

pirical evidence for some of the countries we are interested in, to see how relevant the theories discussed in previous sections might be. In the final section of this chapter we will give a preliminary interpretation of why stagflation was an outcome of the stabilization policies in the Latin American cases that we are considering.

In what follows we will assume that the degree of opening up to the international economy is not important in determining the behavior of the economy. This is a reasonable assumption for most phases in the Latin American stabilization processes since the reduction of high external tariffs and capital liberalization took place gradually. This means that the open economy case was not relevant in terms of adjustment processes until the last phase of the stabilization effort—Chile after 1979, Argentina after 1980.

A Summary of Hypotheses

There are three hypotheses that are useful for understanding the relation between orthodox stabilization policies and stagflation. The first one refers to limited price flexibility. To the second—the origin of inflationary disturbance—it will be argued that in the "new" inflation of the 1970s and 1980s, a significant part of inflationary shocks was generated on the supply side. It will then follow as a third hypothesis that given limited price flexibility and supply inflationary shocks, the use of conventional contractionary demand policies by themselves are likely to generate adjustments that are far from optimal. The economy will react mainly by reducing output (and increasing unemployment) whereas the decrease in the rate of inflation will be more slow to come due to price and wage rigidities and continued cost-push and other pressures on the supply side. This is what we have called the stagflationary effect of the policies.

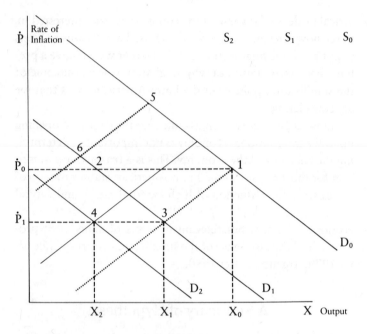

FIGURE 1
Limited Price Flexibility

It might be useful briefly to summarize the arguments before following the discussion in the next section at a more technical level. Let us represent the relationship between the rate of inflation and the level of output in the economy in Figure 1.

D_0 represents aggregate demand in the economy. It can be shifted upward or downward by changes in fiscal or monetary policy. S_0 represents aggregate supply of goods and services in the economy. It reflects cost conditions which vary according to how close (or far) the economy is to fully using its resources—existing capacity and labor.

The issue of price flexibility can be put as follows. If prices are fully flexible, upward and downward, any fall in demand, say, from D_0 to D_1 due to contractionary monetary and fiscal policies, will be met by a rapid reduction in the rate of inflation from P_0 to P_1. There will also be an output reduction from X_0 to X_1. On the other hand, if prices are less than perfectly flexible, the shift in demand from D_0 to D_1 will follow a different path. In Figure 1, it will go from 1 to 2 first and then only slowly will move from 2 to 3. In other words, when demand falls, the adjustment will be produced first by reducing output; and only after enough slack is generated in the economy (and unemployment), will prices gradually start coming down.

We will argue in the next section that there are some good reasons to expect this kind of behavior. There are institutional factors that influence the behavior of labor and goods markets in modern economies that imply, as a consequence, that wages and prices do not adjust instantaneously to demand changes in the short run. This is particularly true in manufacturing, in the public sector, and in modern labor markets.

The reason is that in a frequently changing economic environment, workers and, to some extent, firms develop a preference for stable employment in the short run vis-à-vis changes in demand conditions. Long or medium-term contracts are signed that essentially make wages independent of short-term fluctuations. Since firms determine prices mostly as a markup over costs and wages are the main component in variable costs, prices will, basically, transmit changes in wages. If wages are relatively inflexible downward, prices will also be. This tendency is reinforced when firms are oligopolies, whose long-run interest is price stability, in order to maintain the (implicit or explicit) price agreement with other producers in order to maximize long-term profits.

A hypothesis that is complementary to the previous one refers to the medium-term behavior of wages and prices. If a basic consideration in wage determination under labor contracts is what other workers have obtained in their wage settle-

ments, the labor market as a whole will exhibit permanent disequilibrium because contracts signed at one point in time (say,
during economic expansion) will influence contracts signed at
a later period (say, during a recessionary phase). The net result
will be an upward trend in wage settlements and, consequently,
in prices. Wages show more flexibility upward than downward.
In terms of Figure 1 this will reflect in a slow upward movement of aggregate supply curve from S_0 toward S_1. Under
these conditions, the difficulties in reducing the rate of inflation
by contracting demand will be compounded. In order to reach
the target rate of inflation P_1, output will have to fall from X_0 to
X_2, which is obviously larger than the output reduction from
X_0 to X_1.

A second hypothesis is that the dominant factors behind
inflation changed significantly after the disruptions in world
markets in the early 1970s. Exogenous shocks originating in
the prices of raw materials and in increased external inflation
rendered conventional stabilization policies more ineffective.
In terms of Figure 1 the new inflation would be characterized
by sudden upward shifts in S_0: first to S_1, then to S_2, as a reaction to oil price increases or other exogenous shocks. If this
were the case, it is obvious that demand-side policies (monetary
contraction and reductions in the government deficit) will have
to be administered in larger doses in order to achieve the same
result, like keeping the rate of inflation constant. What one
would observe would be a stable or even increasing rate of inflation (moving from point 1, toward 5 and 6, in Figure 1) and a
deeper recession (output levels falling below X_2). This would
be a typical stagflation resulting from the interaction of institutional factors limiting downward flexibility in wages and prices
with exogenous supply shocks and with the application of one-
sided policies, centered in reducing demand pressures, without
duly considering the other factor just mentioned.

Suppose this is an accurate picture of how modern economies work. How relevant is all this to our study of Latin Ameri-

can stabilization? Although we will discuss this in the last two sections of this chapter, let us give some indication of what is suggested there. One, from what we can learn from scarce empirical studies in Latin America, it seems that these hypotheses would be generally valid for the modern sector of these economies under "normal" conditions. These refer to the normal functioning of markets in the economy. But the stabilization programs of the 1970s in Latin America were characterized by disruption and control of the labor market. Real wages were reduced by administrative decree, and collective bargaining was suppressed. This was a key difference since labor markets seemed to play a central role in the transmission of inflation in industrial countries.

Other differences refer to the greater importance of imported intermediate inputs and working capital as inputs in production, a probably larger significance of oligopolistic behavior in the goods market, and a larger and more permanent disequilibrium affecting most markets. The specific way these particular features affect prices and output will be examined later in this chapter and particularly in Chapter 7.

Limited Downward Flexibility in Prices and Wages

Our first hypothesis is that limited wage and price flexibility is one of the factors explaining the stagflationary effect of demand-contractionary stabilization policies. Why would limited price flexibility be an important characteristic in modern economies? Institutional factors have to do with this phenomenon.[2]

2. See J. Tobin, "Inflation and Unemployment," *American Economic Review,* March 1972. See also O. Eckstein, ed., *The Econometrics of Price Determination* (Board of Governors, Federal Reserve, 1972). See particularly W. Nordhaus, "Recent Development in Price Dynamics," O. Eckstein and D. Wyn, "Industry Price Equations," and J. Tobin, "The Wage-Price Mechanism," all

One such factor would be the predominance of a large segment of the economy where prices are administered, that is, where prices do not respond to short-run changes in demand conditions but are set according to long-run considerations such as "normal" average costs or long-term contracts and the like. This administered-price sector prevails typically in manufacturing, in the public sector, and in the organized labor market. These are often called the fixed-price sectors. The other segment, characterized by perfectly flexible prices (vis-à-vis changes in demand), prevails in agriculture, raw materials, services, and small-scale production activities. They are often referred to as the flexible-price sectors.[3]

The way these two segments of the economy interact is as follows. Suppose a stabilization program is implemented consisting in reducing money supply and government expenditures. As a result of the policy, aggregate demand falls. Firms in the administered sector adjust in the short run by reducing output first while prices react more slowly. Workers are laid off in order to meet lower output requirements, and unemployment goes up. Producers in the flexible-price sector, on the other hand, react to lower demand by rapidly reducing prices and wages. Output and employment levels are not seriously affected. Eventually, some of the unemployed in the fixed-price activities shift to the flexible-price sector where redundant labor depresses real wages even more but employment grows. More workers find jobs at lower average wages. If segmentation between the two markets is serious, the unemployment effect of the recessionary policies is more severe because unemployed labor from the fixed-price sector will not shift to the flexible-price sector. Open unemployment will go up. The op-

three in Eckstein, ed., *Econometrics.* See also W. Godley and W. Nordhaus, "Pricing in the Trade Cycle," *Economic Journal,* Sept. 1972.

3. This argument is developed by W. Nordhaus, "Inflation Theory and Policy," *American Economic Review,* May 1976.

posite situation prevails if the administered-price sector and the flexible-price activities are well integrated. In this case, open unemployment will not increase significantly, but the number of part-time workers in the competitive sector will increase, reducing average income for those employed in these activities. But why would prices exhibit limited flexibility in the so-called administered-price sectors? There are two main sources of price rigidity. One is the structure of the market; the other are institutional factors, like the extended use of long-term contracts in the labor and goods markets.

The structure of the market may influence price behavior. It is a well-documented fact that oligopolistic markets exhibit more limited price flexibility than what is observed in competitive atomistic markets. Oligopolies do not change prices often, certainly not during transitory changes in demand conditions.[4] Noncompetitive firms that are predominant in the manufacturing sector set prices as a markup over "normal" variable costs, that is, those costs reflecting an average level of capacity utilization. Thus, oligopolistic prices, just as administered prices generally, change little during the cycle, except when demand shifts are very large or permanent. In spite of this general rule, price behavior is not entirely symmetrical: in the upswing, when the economy is reaching full capacity, noncompetitive firms are more willing to increase their prices than they are to reduce them in the downswing. In other words, noncompetitive prices are more rigid downward than they are upward.

But there are institutional sources of price rigidity as well. The increased importance of long-term contracts regulating wages and goods' prices for stable customers has become a relatively new feature in modern economies. It has certainly affected price and wage behavior quite independent of market structure (competitive or noncompetitive) or short-term de-

4. A. Leijonhufbud, *On Keynesian Economics and the Economies of Keynes* (Oxford University Press, 1968).

mand conditions. Take, for example, the labor market. Wages in a modern economy are hardly responsive to short-term fluctuations in aggregate demand. This happens in spite of the fact that only a minor fraction of the labor force is unionized, which means that rigid wages are not necessarily imposed by noncompetitive unions but are a part of voluntary agreements between workers and employers. Stable wages are a convenient feature that maximizes workers' welfare and firms' long-run productivity and profits.[5]

This fact is related to specific features of the labor market and production processes in the modern sector of the economy. Jobs offered in the labor market have a certain productivity attached to the job itself, and skills for specific jobs are learned by on-the-job training. On the other hand, workers' productivities are not fixed and entirely predetermined. Hence, for a maximum productivity to be achieved, the voluntary cooperation of workers is essential. At the same time, skills are transferred by a learning process where the newly hired are trained by senior workers. For older workers to be willing to train the newcomers, they must be guaranteed a certain wage, irrespective of demand and output fluctuations—and their job must be safe; that is, if the firm must lay off workers during a recession, it must begin by eliminating the younger members of the work force. Through these means, the firm is guaranteed the maximum voluntary cooperation of the more skilled workers in order to train the younger less skilled entrants in the labor market.

On the other hand, total productivity is not just the sum of individual productivities. It is highly dependent on effective team work. This is stimulated if workers feel that the structure

5. L. Thurow, *The Zero-Sum Society* (Basic Books, 1980); P. Doeringer and M. Piore, *Internal Labor Markets and Manpower Analysis* (Lexington Books, 1971); J. Hicks, *The Crisis in Keynesian Economics* (Oxford University Press, 1974).

of relative wages within the firm and vis-à-vis other firms is fair and reflects the contribution that each worker makes in the production process. Altering this structure in order to adjust to changed demand conditions may result in cost savings, but it will almost certainly have a negative repercussion in the productivity of the firm.

What the previous institutional arrangement leads to is stable wages that are agreed upon by the workers and the firm as part of a long-term labor contract. With stable wages, the firm sets prices as a markup over this variable cost. Prices for individual firms or sectors subject to a certain long-term contract do not fluctuate much during the cycle. They are administered following a pattern set by the underlying long-term contract. These administered prices are independent of market structure although it is generally agreed that the pattern of price rigidity is reinforced in concentrated industries.[6]

If wages and prices are set for a certain period of time, when are they changed? Wages change when contracts are renegotiated and demand conditions have changed in a more permanent manner. Wages also change when contracts are broken due to particularly severe conditions in the economy. Thus, if a drastic monetary contraction sets in a deep recession that increases unemployment several times its normal rate, it is likely that the whole institution of labor contracts as well as the relative wage structure will collapse.

The other element performing a key role in labor market behavior, besides the existence of labor contracts, is the relative wage structure. Workers will negotiate a labor contract, having in mind what workers in other industries are getting for similar jobs. If contracts are not negotiated simultaneously, this will introduce permanent disequilibrium in the labor market. At one point in time some workers are negotiating based on pre-

6. Tobin, "Inflation and Unemployment."

vious agreements by other workers. The new contract will affect other workers' contracts in the future and so on.

When some negotiations take place in the upper part of the cycle (aggregate demand and sales are expanding), it is likely that a generous wage settlement will be obtained. Through the structure of relative wages, the high wage settlement will permeate wage negotiations for firms or sectors whose contracts are due when the economy is in a downswing. Thus, it will induce a higher wage settlement during the recession than otherwise. The high wage increase will be transferred to prices through the markup rule. The net result of the process will be persistent inflation in spite of general recessionary conditions.[7]

What if not only the labor market is in disequilibrium but the goods market as well? As will be shown in Chapter 7, market disequilibrium can only add to price rigidity. When firms are facing uncertainty and market disequilibrium, they refrain from adjusting prices downward when demand falls, lest they mistake other firms' reactions and end up decreasing profit margins without gaining new customers. Under these conditions, Arrow has shown, all firms behave as if in imperfect competition.[8] They become price setters. Because information is imperfect and uncertain, firms will change prices slowly even when demand conditions have sharply deteriorated, as in a policy-induced recession.

Supply Shocks

Besides the institutional features noted above, new factors have been present in the world economy since the early seventies that have aggravated the inflationary problem

7. See J. Tobin, "Stabilization Policy Ten Years After," *Brookings Papers on Economic Activity,* No. 1, 1980.
8. K. Arrow, "Toward a Theory of Price Adjustments," in M. Abramovitz, ed., *The Allocation of Economic Resources* (Stanford University Press, 1959).

and have rendered conventional stabilization policies even more ineffective in dealing with it.

Price rigidity in the administered-price sector has been accompanied by external shocks originating mainly in the flexible-price sector. It is the international price of food, energy, and raw materials that has increased sharply and discontinuously due to a number of unpredictable events like bad crops, cartel agreements, and raw materials scarcity.

External price shocks have been internalized mostly in terms of higher domestic inflation and partly in terms of lower output and higher unemployment. The direct effect of higher external prices is that of reducing the purchasing power of domestically generated production and income but not necessarily of reducing production in physical terms. But an indirect effect is that, given global supply constraints, unless the largest consumers (the industrial countries) reduce their demand by slowing down their growth rates, new price increases will follow.[9] Slower growth in the industrial economies sets a worldwide recessionary tendency. Thus, the original price hike results in idle capacity and unemployment in most economies.

Another indirect effect of the "new inflation" generated by supply shocks is that if it is dealt with by conventional demand management policies, it will result mostly in recession and unemployment, and inflationary pressures will not be abated to a significant extent. If every time an external shock occurs, the monetary authority reacts by deflating the economy, excess capacity and unemployment will become a more or less permanent feature. Given limited downward flexibility in prices and exogenous price shocks, permanent recession will most likely be accompanied by permanent inflation.

How can a situation like this be dealt with? There are three possible courses of action: to accommodate the external shocks, to engineer a recession as large as necessary to compen-

9. Tobin, "Stabilization Policy."

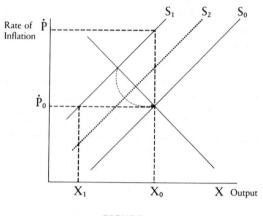

FIGURE 2
Supply Shocks

sate for the upward pressure in prices, or to deal with the problem from the supply side, that is, by applying supply "disinflationary shocks."[10] These three possibilities are illustrated in Figure 2.

The exogenous supply shock, like an increase in the price of oil, is shown by the upward shift in the supply curve from S_0 to S_1. Costs are now higher per unit of output. Prices are increased according to the markup rule.

The first adjustment possibility is an accommodation to higher external prices. It means compensating for the potential unemployment effect of the price shock by expanding the level of expenditures. Sectors that might be hard hit by the higher external prices and that consequently would reduce output and lay off workers are directly subsidized by the government. The policy avoids unemployment but internalizes a higher rate of

10. The expression is from A. Okun and G. Perry, "Innovative Policies to Slow Inflation," *Brookings Papers on Economic Activity,* No. 2, 1978.

inflation. Output stays constant at X_0, but the rate of inflation goes up from P_0 to P_1 (see Figure 2).

A second policy would consist in trying to maintain the rate of inflation prevailing before the price shock by reducing expenditures. In this case most of the adjustment will come through output and employment reduction while the rate of inflation will converge to the original lower level slowly due to the institutional and structural rigidities for the downward movement of prices and wages that we referred to in the previous section. Output will go down from X_0 to X_1 in order to maintain the rate of inflation constant at $\dot{P}_0$ in the face of the external shock (see Figure 2).

A third type of policies would consist in dealing with the problem from the supply side, where in fact it originated. Three main alternatives seem to be available here. One is to administer supply "disinflationary shocks," compensating higher costs by reducing such domestic cost components as production taxes, social security contributions, or wages. A second one is to put the emphasis in productivity increases as a way of counteracting the upward trend in variable costs. This is the rationale for business tax reductions and investment incentives policy that is so much a part of so-called supply-side economics. The third alternative is to neutralize the acceleration in the rate of cost and price increases by a consistent application of an incomes policy that would "guide" wages and prices downward so that the cost of adjustment to higher raw materials prices is evenly distributed between wage and profit earners. The effect of any of these courses of action is to shift the supply curve from S_1 gradually to S_0. The path toward the original level of inflation and output $\dot{P}_0$ and X_0 is probably less costly in terms of time and output losses.

In sum, (1) the structure of modern economies is characterized by the existence of a large segment of the economy where prices and wages are administered, that is, they are set through a variety of institutional mechanisms independently of short-term demand conditions;[11] (2) prices in the administered sector are fixed by firms as a markup over long-run "normal" variable costs, and wages as a function of relative wages in other firms and sectors and of expected inflation; (3) this kind of price and wage setting in a modern economy, where the administered-price sector is predominant, has two consequences: given that prices and wages are not influenced by short-run demand changes, a policy of demand contraction, as orthodox stabilization policies are, will not affect prices and wages in a significant manner, in the short run.[12] Another consequence is that since wages depend on relative earnings elsewhere, it suffices that some firms obtain a generous wage settlement for this to start a chain reaction demanding higher wages in other sectors. Wages are more flexible in an upward than in a downward direction; and (4) external price shocks, like those experienced in the 1970s and 1980s in the world economy, by increasing costs, make the process of adjustment through the demand side even more costly.

The Latin American Context

We are now in a position to discuss the relevance of the interpretative frameworks for the Latin American economies. In order to do this, we must rely on accumulated

11. For theoretical implications of administered prices in the behavior of the economy, see E. Malinvaud, *The Theory of Unemployment Reconsidered* (Halsted Press, 1977); and R. Barro and H. Grossman, "A General Disequilibrium Model of Income and Employment," *American Economic Review*, March 1971.

12. It will reduce prices and wages in the competitive, flexible-price segment of the economy (primary sectors and services), but it is the fixed-price sector that predominates and extends more rapidly in modern economies; see Tobin, "Inflation and Unemployment."

knowledge of the specific characteristics of these economies vis-à-vis the developed economies and on empirical studies that deal with the issues that we have been discussing in previous sections. Most of these empirical studies refer to the 1950s and 1960s when the economies were functioning under "normal" conditions in the sense that no serious market disruptions were present nor radical institutional reforms governing the functioning of the economy were enforced. Thus, the discussion in this section refers only to studies covering that period. A hypothesis of how these conditions might have changed during the neoconservative experiments of the 1970s will be developed in the final section of this chapter.

Generally accepted descriptions of economies in Latin America in the 1960s would include a modern sector that consists of a rather well-developed manufacturing sector and a large public sector. Labor markets in these activities would be well organized, with powerful labor unions and frequent sectoral wage negotiations taking place.

Empirical evidence, scarce as it is, seems to suggest that the modern sector in these economies would behave not too differently from the so-called administered-price sector. Industrial prices appear to be determined as a markup over variable costs, including labor, imported input costs, and the cost of domestic capital.[13] Demand effects on wages or prices do not seem to be significant.[14] Wages are mainly but not exclusively a function

13. J. Behrman, "Econometric Modeling of National Income Determination in Latin America," *Annals of Economic and Social Measurement* (NBER) 4 (1975); V. Corbo, *Inflation in Developing Countries* (Amsterdam: North Holland, 1974).

14. R. Cortázar, "Salarios industriales en el corto plazo: Chile," CIEPLAN (mimeo), Nov. 1980; T. Reichman, *Inflación y economía chilena,* Publication No. 14, Economics Department, University of Chile, 1974; M. Brodersohn, "La curva de Phillips y el conflicto entre el pleno empleo y la estabilidad de precios en Argentina 1964–1974," Documento de trabajo, Instituto Torcuato di Tella, Buenos Aires, 1975.

of expected inflation as reflected by past price increases. Although unemployment does not show a significant effect on wages in these empirical studies, there is some evidence supporting an institutional factor in wage determination. Cortázar finds evidence in favor of a "wage contours hypothesis," that is, that wages depend on wage settlements obtained in key sectors or enterprises. His study shows the public sector performing the leading role in wage settlements.[15] Brodersohn finds a "union strength" factor to be significant in Argentina.[16]

One differentiating element with respect to industrial countries is the importance of imported inputs and working capital (besides wages) as cost-push factors. At the same time, empirical evidence suggests that the relative autonomy of prices and wages vis-à-vis short-term demand conditions is sustained. On the other hand, institutional factors like relative earnings, wage contours, and leading sectors seem to play a role in wage determination in the modern sector of the economy. The administered-price hypothesis is also supported on the price side, given evidence that suggests that prices in the industrial sector are set as a markup over variable costs with a weak effect from the demand side.[17]

On the other hand, traditional activities in Latin American economies would probably correspond more closely to a flexible-price sector. Traditional agriculture, small-scale production, and services would be sectors where demand changes should be readily reflected in prices, and to a lesser extent in wages. A tightening of demand should result in lower prices rather than extensive unemployment. Unfortunately, empirical studies do not usually include these activities so that the previous hypothesis is only speculative although it does reflect

15. Cortázar, "Salaros industriales."
16. Brodersohn, "La curva de Phillips."
17. Behrman, "Economic Modeling."

conventional wisdom regarding the behavior of the traditional sector.

The economies of Argentina, Brazil, Chile, and Uruguay are among the most developed in Latin America and, in fact, within developing countries generally. They are characterized by a well-developed manufacturing sector, by an extended and significant public sector, and, except during the current experiments in neoconservative economies, by organized and strong labor unions.

In sum, they belong to the semi-industrialized category where modern sector activities tend to predominate over traditional sector. Thus, limited price and wage flexibility is not a marginal phenomenon but one that is probably significant in explaining the high, persistent inflation that has characterized the economies of Latin America.

Another important specific characteristic of these countries is that their economies are subject to exogenous shocks that tend to be more frequent and intense than in industrial countries. This is due to instability in the international price of the major export product, besides sudden changes in the price of imported inputs. Both factors have been a permanent source of "unexpected" external shocks that forces the devaluation and the deflation of the economy if inflation is to be kept under control, or the borrowing and expanding of wages and expenditures if recession and unemployment are to be avoided. The recurrent cyclical behavior of the Argentinian economy throughout the postwar period is illustrative of the problem,[18] as well as the fluctuations in Chile's GDP due to variations in the international price of copper.

---

18. M. Diamand, "Toward a Change in the Economic Paradigm Through the Experience of Developing Countries," *Journal of Development Economics* 5(1) (1978).

A Preliminary Interpretation of Recent Neoconservative Stabilization Experiments in Latin America

What has been described above corresponds to what is suggested by available empirical studies about the "normal" functioning of economies like those in Latin America, "normal" referring to observed patterns in the postwar period. But in the 1970s, new military governments in Argentina, Chile, and Uruguay initiated an attempt at radical economic reform from the Right. In fact, deep institutional reforms modified the scenario within which economic policies were applied. Perhaps the most radically modified was the functioning of the labor market. Political repression, suppression of collective bargaining, and a drastic fall in demand and real wages had the effect of all but destroying the elaborate system of wage negotiations and contracts. Wages were controlled by decree and maintained at low real levels. In this way the labor sector automatically became an important adjustment factor in the stabilization program. When contrasted with the policy at the other end of the market, which consisted in freeing up goods prices, it is clear that the brunt of the adjustment cost in terms of real income losses was suffered by wage earners.

Market liberalization, on the other hand, proceeded in most other markets. Not only goods prices were deregulated, but the financial and external sectors were liberalized. Interest rates were freed, exchange rate controls partially eliminated, and an opening up of the economy to external trade and financial flows initiated. All these changes occurred in a highly inflationary environment and, in the recent cases of Argentina, Chile, and Uruguay, in the midst of deep changes in the international economy. External price shocks became more frequent and intense, and the private international capital markets expanded after the oil crisis, making the access to external borrowing easy and almost unconstrained.

This is the scenario in which radical orthodox stabilization policies are applied. They all share a concern for bringing demand in line with production by tightening money supply, reducing real wages, and balancing the budget. But different degrees of orthodoxy in practice make for significant variations in the policy mix actually chosen in constrain demand. And, as will be illustrated in Chapter 7, the effects are quite dissimilar, according to the particular package chosen.

Without stressing at this point specific differences, a "stylized" description of a typical stabilization process would be as follows. The contraction of demand happens simultaneously with a strong policy-induced supply shock that is going to alter the whole course of the stabilization program. The supply shock consists in prices being suddenly deregulated after a long period of repressed inflation and substantial instability in most economic indicators. Under such an uncertain and volatile environment, prices overshoot any conceivable equilibrium level (see Chapter 7). The price explosion is reinforced and made more permanent by indexation of most input prices (exchange rate, public utility rates, and public enterprise tariffs).

The price overshoot happens because firms react by increasing markups in order to protect themselves from higher expected inflation and the risk of income losses from such an uncertain and risky environment.

In some cases the policy-induced price shock is made worse by external events: the increase in imported input prices brought about by the oil crisis. Given the reinforcing pattern of supply-generated price shocks, the supply effect may dominate over contractionary demand policies. The result would be powerful cost pressures followed by an acceleration of inflation. Since money income growth is being constrained by the demand-centered stabilization effort and inflation unexpectedly accelerates, real aggregate demand falls well beyond programed levels. The economy will enter a recession. Accelerated inflation and recession coexist.

The interesting aspect in this process is that prices are not driven up by wages as assumed by standard macroeconomic theory. It must be remembered that wage determination played a key role in the interpretation of inflation in industrial countries. Wage increases were negotiated considering expected future inflation and the relative position of workers in one firm or sector vis-à-vis others. There are abundant reasons for price expectations and relative wages to vary frequently in the modern administered-price sector of an economy, and this seemed to be an important source of inflation. Firms in this context merely transmit wage increases toward prices through a simple markup rule.

What happens when this mechanism is not present—because collective bargaining does not exist—labor unions are not allowed to function, and nominal wages are fixed by decree, usually resulting in sharp real wage reductions? What drives prices up? A part of the explanation may lie in the fact that wages are not the only relevant variable costs considered by firms when setting prices. In countries where external sector imbalances are chronic, domestic capital markets are undeveloped, and raw material prices are highly unstable—as argued in the previous section—the exchange rate, the cost of domestic capital, and raw material prices become important elements influencing the rate of change in prices. Large devaluations will increase the cost of essential imported inputs. Capital market liberalization will push interest rates up with significant effect on the price level. These mechanisms—analyzed in more detail in Chapter 7—probably played a part in the persistence of inflation in spite of restrictive monetary and fiscal policies.

But another critical element that to some extent differentiates these cases from more conventional stabilization "stories" in the industrial countries is that price decisions by firms in the administered-price sector seem to play an active role in fueling the inflationary process. If administered prices are no longer the mere passive reflection of events in the labor market or inputs market, they might become an autonomous force behind inflation. As Frenkel has suggested, in an uncertain environment of very high inflation, firms may increase prices in the short run more than proportionately with respect to cost increases in order to protect themselves from the risks of unexpected losses due to wrong predictions about future inflation.[19] This reaction by firms becomes more important the more scarce the information available about expected prices and the more costly it is to obtain it. Highly uncertain economic environments also reinforce the tendency of firms to increase markups in the short run in order to hedge against unexpected price increases elsewhere in the economy.

Double or three-digit inflation, as observed in Argentina, Chile, and Uruguay before and during the first years of the stabilization program, provides the kind of environment where imperfect information, uncertainty about future inflation, and the high risk attached to them become determining elements in price decisions by firms. Markups become a function of expected inflation scaled up by an uncertainty and risk premium. During the period of high inflation, maximum uncertainty, and market disequilibrium, prices exhibit some autonomy not only from demand but also from cost increases. Empirical evidence for Argentina and Chile makes this interpretation a reasonable one.[20]

In sum, if there is a combined effect of high inflationary expectations-cum-indexation, significant cost increases due to devaluation, financial liberalization, external price shocks, and

19. R. Frenkel, "Decisiones de precio en alta inflación,"*Estudios CEDES* (Buenos Aires) 2(3) (1979), demonstrates this point.

20. Ibid.; J. Ramos, "Inflación persistente, inflación reprimida e hiperestanflación," *Cuadernos de Economía,* No. 43, 1977.

higher markups in the administered-price sector during the first phase of the stabilization program, it is very likely that the inflationary process will be dominated by supply-side effects. It is not surprising then that stabilization policies that were focused on curbing demand were slow in reducing inflation. And yet they rapidly generated recessionary conditions in the economy. The adjustment process was long and costly.

This brief preliminary interpretation of the orthodox stabilization process would not be complete without referring to the role of monetary policy. Money supply has often been a passive variable in Latin America, adapting to impulses emanating from the public and external sectors. In spite of a more deliberate attempt at making money supply an effective policy instrument during recent orthodox stabilization experiments in Latin America, results have not been very successful, as will be shown in the next chapter. Beyond traditional factors like unexpected fluctuations in export earnings due to price variations and fiscal deficits, new policy-created factors have been present. Among these, financial liberalization plays a very significant role because it creates money substitutes that increase money supply beyond programed and controllable levels. External financial opening results in unexpectedly large accumulation of reserves with an additional expansionary effect on money supply. During the transition, when the economy is still not fully open, these new factors may weaken the core of orthodox stabilization. Monetary control may lose much of its effectiveness as an instrument for stopping inflation.

7

Adjustment Processes
for Economic Stabilization

HERE we will deal in more detail with the specific economic adjustment processes chosen to bring the economy back to equilibrium in recent and current experiences in Latin America. By studying each policy instrument separately, we will attempt to trace the impact of each of them on inflation, output, and employment.

The description of the adjustment processes will reflect stylized facts rather than any particular country's experience. It will also concentrate selectively on just a few of these mechanisms of adjustment—the criterion for selecting these and not others being that they seem particularly relevant for explaining the stagflation that accompanied these experiences.

Three main policy actions constituted the basis of the monetarist stabilization program. The first was to depress aggregate demand by enforcing contractionary monetary and fiscal policies. In terms of Figure 3, the objective of these policies was to reduce inflation from $\dot{P}_0$ to $\dot{P}_1$ by shifting D_0 down to D_1. In the next two sections, we will argue that monetary policy was not used very effectively and that fiscal discipline, although more effective, tended to produce negative income distribution effects.

A second set of policy actions referred to adjustments in relative prices. Price deregulation, including interest rates, and exchange rate devaluations were undertaken as a way of restoring efficient market allocation mechanisms and equilibrat-

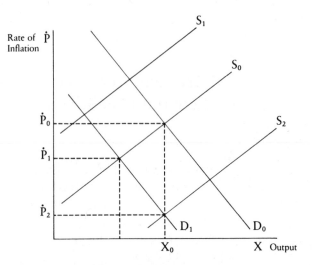

FIGURE 3
Depressing Aggregate Demand

ing the balance of payments. We will suggest in the next three sections that an important indirect effect of freeing up prices and the interest rate and of sharply devaluing domestic currency was to create powerful cost pressures that were equivalent to supply shocks in the economy. In terms of Figure 3, the effect of the policies was to shift aggregate supply upward from S_0 to S_1 due to the sudden cost increase produced by price deregulation and devaluation.

A third policy action consisted in opening up the economy to trade and financial flows. This was part of the structural transformation of the economy within the context of the neoconservative program. But it also had the objective of providing an additional mechanism to bring the rate of inflation down. With low tariffs and liberalization of external capital flows, domestic inflation rates should converge toward the lower international rate. This should happen, among other mechanisms, because of the "law of one price" and because of interest rate equalization between domestic and external markets. In other words, as a result of these policy actions, S_1 in Figure 3 would gradually shift back toward S_2, a level of supply that would presumably be consistent with equilibrium at the world rate of inflation. The effective role played by the opening up policy as a stabilization instrument is discussed in the last two sections of this chapter.

Monetary Control

Decreasing the rate of expansion of money supply is perhaps the main policy objective in conventional monetarism. It was certainly so in the stabilization programs of Brazil, Argentina, Uruguay, and Chile in the period under study. And yet, in spite of sustained efforts on the part of monetary authorities in these countries, the rate of growth of money supply only gradually decreased, as indeed data in Figures 4 and 5 show. It has been argued that this demonstrates that these programs cannot be called monetarists since the basic policy action—sharply tightening money supply—was not accomplished.[1]

The argument is valid in a purely formal sense. As Tobin has stated:

The practice of describing monetary policy in terms of observed growth rates of M_i is misleading. It does not make sense to say that the policy was or is X percent money stock growth as if that number were something the central bank chooses arbitrarily and gratui-

1. See A. Harberger, "Comments" to A. Foxley, "Stabilization Policies and Their Effects on Employment and Income Distribution," in W. Cline and S. Weintraub, eds., *Economic Stabilization in Developing Countries* (Brookings Institution, 1981).

tously.... When the authorities have chosen policies supportive of continued inflationary growth of M·V, they have not done so from ignorance of arithmetic, indifference to inflation, or, in my opinion, political pressure. They have done so, rightly or wrongly, mainly because of the perceived consequences of nonaccommodation on the real performance of the economy. The inertia of inflation in the face of nonaccommodative policies is the big issue. To discuss the roots of that inertia and the sources of nonmonetary pressures for accommodation—administered prices, contracts, collective bargaining, distributive conflict, supply shocks, OPEC—is not to commit any vulgar errors or to violate any of the identities stipulated above.[2]

This states the real issue behind any monetarist program: the grave difficulties encountered by a nonaccommodative monetary policy due to inflationary inertia. Monetary policy may be largely nonaccommodative, but it cannot be totally nonaccommodative, particularly in the context of a semi-industrialized economy.

Suppose the stabilization program does the following things at the same time: it reduces government expenditures and credit expansion, it devalues the currency in order to bring the external accounts into balance, and it deregulates prices so that efficient allocation of resources is possible. These policies will probably have the effect of reducing nominal aggregate demand, of overexpanding prices, and consequently of producing a sudden fall in real aggregate demand in spite of moderate reductions in the rate of expansion in money supply. Under these conditions, the economy will enter a recession in spite of high inflation. Figures for Chile in 1975 are an extreme case but illustrative of the point. The GDP fell by 10% (net of the effect

2. J. Tobin, "Stabilization Policy Ten Years After," *Brookings Papers on Economic Activity*, No. 1, 1980.

of lower copper prices), unemployment went up to 19% in the last quarter, and still prices grew by 343% and the money supply by 265%. This may not look like a monetary crunch in nominal terms, but it certainly was one in real terms; real cash balances decreased by 33% between 1974 and 1975.[3]

Once the price overshoot occurred and all the rest followed, the monetary authority was faced with the alternative of reducing nominal supply even more, that is, to a rate below 265%. This can only happen at the expense of a GDP reduction beyond 10% and unemployment higher than 19%. Even in an authoritarian context, there is a limit to nonaccommodation in a monetary policy!

If one source of inflationary inertia is repressed inflation, other sources of a more general nature are the fiscal deficit and public enterprises deficits. To the extent that additional unemployment beyond that created by the contraction of real cash balances is not desired, some graduality is imposed in the reduction of the public deficit. For example, it is this imposed graduality in the reduction of the public deficit plus the price overshoot and inflationary inertia that explains a monetary growth of 311% during 1974 in Chile, in spite of a declared objective of tight money, as a key element in the stabilization program. Thus, indexation of key prices (and contracts) was also a factor that forced some monetary accommodation in the economy, irrespective of declared intentions of the staunchest of monetarists.

If prices of key export commodities fluctuate sharply and frequently—for example coffee in Brazil, beef in Argentina and Uruguay, and copper in Chile—unexpected changes in reserves occur, and they often have, given imperfect sterilization mecha-

3. These figures and those for Brazil that follow are taken from A. Foxley, "Stabilization Policies and Stagflation: The Cases of Brazil and Chile," in A. Foxley and L. Whitehead, eds., *Economic Stabilization in Latin America: Political Dimensions* (Pergamon, 1980).

nisms, an undesired monetary effect. Episodes like the abnormally high price of coffee (and good harvest) in Brazil in 1965 were directly related to an unexpected 80% expansion in money supply, which, compared with the 30% that had been programed, may look like poor performance indeed. But that result was not achieved because of a lack of monetarist conviction, as then Finance Minister Roberto Campos would argue! What happened is that behind the expansion of money supply were factors, like sudden price changes in the main export crop, that could not be easily controlled by policymakers in the short run.

Difficulties in achieving the targets in the reduction of nominal money supply were also the result of policy-created constraints in the cases that we are considering. The creation of money substitutes by private financial institutions encouraged but not controlled by the government in Brazil, Chile, and Argentina, at the same time that M_1 growth rates were being reduced, did not help in the stabilization effort. This factor alone added more than twenty points to the annual rates of expansion of money supply in Chile during the critical shock period. On the other hand, the opening up to external capital flows proved to be an insurmountable obstacle to monetary restraint during the transition from the closed to the open economy. It has become the main factor of monetary expansion in Chile since 1976 and in Argentina since 1977. We will discuss this in more detail in the next sections.

In conclusion, simple, abstract monetarism when confronted with the reality of inflationary inertia, exogenous shocks, and reserve accumulation (plus unexpected results like a price overshoot when prices are deregulated) will almost necessarily turn into a policy of gradual reduction in the rate of growth of money supply. This is not due to the absence of monetary control—it still is the basic policy objective—but rather to institutional and structural constraints that have much to do with the way real economies function.

Fiscal Adjustment

The public sector deficit has been an important source of monetary expansion in Latin America for a long time. During stabilization attempts—particularly those centered on the reduction of money supply—policymakers have given a high priority to balancing fiscal accounts. Figures for Brazil, Uruguay, and Chile, given in Table 29, show a uniform pattern of reduction in the public deficit during the years corresponding to the orthodox stabilization programs.

But there are many alternative ways in which the fiscal deficit can be reduced: by increasing taxation or by emphasizing cuts in government expenditures. Among the latter, there is a choice between reducing current expenditures or public investment. The choice of instruments will probably be influenced not only by short-term considerations but also by the role assigned to the state in the long-term development strategy. Brazil chose to expand the public sector whereas Chile favored its drastic reduction.

These two different long-term models have very different implications for fiscal policies. Brazil chose to reduce the fiscal deficit by increasing taxes and reducing current government expenditures.[4] At the same time, public investment expanded. For example, in 1965 and in the middle of a recession, when industrial production was falling by 4.7%, investment by the central government increased by 8% and that of public enterprises by 70%. This countercyclical policy no doubt helped in terms of lowering unemployment during the recession.[5]

Fiscal adjustment in the Chilean case came mainly through a reduction in public expenditures. Government expenditures

4. Tax revenues increased from 7.8% of GNP in 1963 to 11.1% in 1966.
5. See J. R. Wells, "Growth and Fluctuations in the Brazilian Manufacturing Sector During the 1960s and Early 1970s," Ph.D. diss., Cambridge University, 1977.

TABLE 29
Fiscal Deficit:
Argentina, Brazil, Chile and Uruguay
(percentage of GDP)

ARGENTINA			BRAZIL	
Year	Public Sector Deficit (1)		Year	Federal Government Deficit (2)
1972	2.7		1963	4.2
1973	5.5		1964	3.2
1974	6.2		1965	1.6
1975	11.9		1966	1.1
1976	8.2		1967	1.7
1977	4.2		1968	1.2
1978	3.4		1969	0.6
			1970	0.4

CHILE			URUGUAY	
Year	Fiscal Deficit (3)		Year	Central Government Deficit (4)
1970	2.9		1970	1.8
1971	9.3		1971	5.7
1972	10.5		1972	2.6
1973	8.8		1973	1.4
1974	8.0		1974	4.3
1975	2.9		1975	4.3
1976	2.0		1976	2.6
1977	1.5		1977	1.3
1978	0.8			

Sources:

A. Canitrot and R. Frenkel, "Estabilización y largo plazo: La experiencia argentina 1976–1979," CEDES (mimeo), Buenos Aires, June 1979. For Chile and Brazil, see A. Foxley, "Stabilization Policies and Stagflation: The Cases of Brazil and Chile," *World Development* 8 (1980). Uruguay figures are based on "Un nuevo ensayo de reajuste económico: Uruguay 1974–1979," CINVE, Montevideo, Dec. 1980.

decreased from 29.1% in 1974 to 22% in 1977.[6] At the same time, the share of public investment in GDP fell from 11.8% to 6.3% between the same years. During a critical period of the stabilization program—1975—public investment fell by 48% in real terms. A large part of this was investment in public works and housing, a highly labor-intensive activity, that contracted by 50% in real terms in just one year. This particular fiscal policy contributed to the 20% unemployment rate observed in early 1976 in Chile.

The distributive consequences of the fiscal adjustment are very different according to the instruments chosen. When the adjustment implies a drastic reduction in public expenditures, activities that have a progressive effect on income distribution are bound to be affected. This is the case with expenditures in health, education, housing, and social security. In the Chilean case, public expenditure in these sectors decreased from $90 per person in 1970 to $70 in 1976. On the other hand, reducing public investment in infrastructure had a high unemployment effect that fell most heavily on unskilled or semiskilled laborers.[7]

The other side of fiscal adjustment is taxation, and most countries will make an effort to increase tax revenues as a way of reducing the public deficit. But there are alternatives here also. Just to follow the previous example, let us look at the way tax revenues were increased in Chile after 1974. The main source was the establishment of a value-added tax with a uniform rate of 20%. At the same time several taxes were eliminated altogether: the net wealth tax, the capital gains tax, and the tax on interest payments. Through these changes, direct taxes reduced their share from 33.4% of the total in 1974 to 26.6% in 1977 whereas indirect taxes increased from 66.6% to 73.4%.

6. See A. Foxley and J. P. Arellano, "El Estado y las desigualdades sociales," *Mensaje* No. 261, Aug. 1977.
7. Unemployment for construction workers in Chile was 31% during 1975 and 34% in 1976.

The illustration with the Chilean case is useful in order to stress the cumulative effects that a certain chosen adjustment for the fiscal accounts may have in terms of employment and income distribution. Most distributive signs seem to be negative in this particular case, but it need not be so generally.

What the previous discussion amounts to is that given a target reduction in the fiscal deficit, there are a number of different ways to achieve this objective. The equity and employment implications of each one are also very different, as our discussion has suggested.

Why would policymakers not always choose that package that has the least negative distributive impact? We have suggested that the answer lies in the nature of the long-term development model and the role assigned within it to the various economic agents. If, for example, the model postulates a reduced public sector and an increased role for private capital, as the neoconservative program does, then it is likely that this will be reflected in fiscal, as in other areas of policy. This policy orientation may imply negative distributive effects. To the extent that the conflict is solved in favor of a larger control over resources by private capital at the expense of equity, this only confirms the preeminence of the privatization objective over others.

Deregulation of Prices

Having examined the role and effect of policy actions oriented toward reducing aggregate demand, let us turn now to those policies designed to affect relative prices and restore market mechanisms. Let us assume that the economy is initially in a state of disequilibrium, characterized by repressed inflation. A generalized system of price controls does not allow the market to provide the right signals so that equilibrium can be restored. As a result, goods are scarce and black markets develop.

Suddenly prices are set free. If nominal wages are fixed, a first impact of price deregulation will be that real wages will fall. When prices are set too high and wages too low, an excess supply of goods will tend to develop, whose final effect might very well be a reduction in output levels and an increase in unemployment, with a probable regressive effect on the distribution of income. In what follows, we will examine these arguments in more detail.

When prices are suddenly freed after a period of repressed inflation, producers must make decisions concerning output and prices. Information about the future is highly imperfect at this time. The market provides no uniform guide. The rate of price increase expected by the various economic agents differs markedly, as well as the expectations about the set of relative prices that each will face.

The variance of expected inflation tends to be higher the higher the inherited disequilibrium is. Under these conditions—extreme uncertainty and expected large price increases—firms will attempt to protect themselves from the risks of huge losses attached to an underestimation of future inflation. One way they could do this is by setting prices initially at a higher level than what they expect inflation to be.[8] Thus, because of a lack of adequate market signals and a high variance of expectations, there will be a tendency for a price overshoot to occur.[9]

8. Frenkel has developed a mathematical model that shows this as a rational outcome for firms facing high inflation and uncertainty; see R. Frenkel, "Decisiones de precio en alta inflación," *Estudios CEDES* 2(3) (1979).

9. Ramos was the first to describe this phenomenon in the case of Chile. His "Hyperstagflation" has certainly been influential in my own thinking about the importance of the initial price overshoot; see J. Ramos "Inflación persistente, inflación reprimida e hiperestanflación," *Cuadernos de Economía*, No. 43, 1977.

TABLE 30

Prices, Money Supply, and
Exchange Rate Increases: Argentina
(Index December 1970 = 1)

Date	Prices (1)	Money (M$_2$) (2)	Exchange Rate (3)
June 1976	55.0	35.1	53.6
December 1976	89.4	74.6	69.3
December 1977	232.8	241.7	153.2
December 1978	628.0	656.7	261.3

Source:
A. Canitrot and R. Frenkel, "Estabilización y largo plazo: La experiencia argentina 1976–1979," CEDES (mimeo), Buenos Aires, June 1979.

TABLE 31

Prices, Money Supply, and
Exchange Rate Increases: Chile
(Index December 1969 = 1)

Date	Prices (1)	Money (M$_2$) (2)	Exchange Rate (3)
Oct.–Dec. 1973	41.7	29.5	30.6
December 1974	205.3	118.0	163.2
December 1975	910.3	507.1	831.7
December 1976	2,712.1	1,912.5	1,716.7
December 1977	4,996.2	5,015.0	2,781.3

Source:
J. Ramos, "Inflación persistente, inflación reprimida e hiperestanflación," *Cuadernos de Economía,* No. 43, 1977.

This is not just an abstract speculation. It is what figures show for at least two of the cases that have been considered, as can be seen in Tables 30 and 31. In Argentina, after three months of free prices (June 1976) the general price level had increased fifty-five times with respect to a normal period (December 1970). Money supply had increased only thirty-five times and the exchange rate fifty-three times during the same period.

The picture for the Chilean economy looks very similar. While prices rose forty-two times between the last three months of 1973 (the period when prices were decontrolled) and a normal period (December 1969), money supply and the exchange rate had grown only by thirty-one times, and wages, although not shown in Table 31, had grown only by twenty-four times. This trend persisted for a sustained period thereafter.

Why would this initial overshoot in prices generate more than a once-and-for-all effect that should be rapidly corrected by market forces? Part of the explanation lies in expectation formation. In fact, the fast pace of price increases that follows decontrol sets a benchmark that influences inflationary expectations. What happens is that after the initial upsurge in the prices of goods, other prices, like the nominal interest rate, the exchange rate, and utilities rates, will tend to be readjusted in proportion to the initial price increase. This affects the costs of imported raw materials, domestic inputs, and working capital. If firms determine prices as a markup over variable costs, a second round of price increases will follow. This way the initial disequilibrium is passed on through the "indexation" it induces in the prices of those variables most determinant of firms' variable costs.

On the other hand, simultaneous with the price overshoot, nominal wages are fixed and the rate of expansion of money supply is falling, as part of the demand-centered stabilization effort. What follows is a significant drop in effective demand.

The overshoot in prices makes real wages and real cash balances fall well beyond what had originally been programed.[10] We now have an income-constrained adjustment process. Producers and consumers alike cannot realize their "notional" demands. Their market signals correspond to a level of effective demand below the potential level. Resources are underutilized. An excess supply of goods develops and is transmitted to the labor market as a reduced demand for labor. This generates excess labor supply, which in turn reduces effective demand again. Income falls. Unemployment goes up.[11]

The drop in demand should eventually have an effect on curbing the rate of price increase. But the speed with which this will happen depends on several factors, and my hypothesis is that the price adjustment process will tend to be slow. One reason for this is that firms are continuously facing changed initial conditions that represent disequilibrium in other markets.

Another reason is that after the initial price overshoot and consequent departure further away from equilibrium, firms do not behave as atomistic competitors but rather as an oligopoly. The reasons for this kind of behavior under disequilibrium have been extensively developed by several authors.[12]

The argument runs as follows: with imperfect information and no market auctioneer, departures from equilibrium imply that firms are necessarily price setters. Since information is imperfect, their profits will depend on other firms' and consumers' reaction to their own pricing and output decisions. They face a demand curve whose slope is not known.

10. See J. Ramos, "El costo social: Hechos e interpretaciones," *Estudios de Economía,* University of Chile, 2nd semester, 1975.

11. This kind of dynamic adjustment is fully described in A. Leijonhufbud, *On Keynesian Economics and the Economies of Keynes* (Oxford University Press, 1968); see also J. Muellbauer and R. Portes, "Macroeconomic Models with Quantity Rationing," *Economic Journal,* Dec. 1978.

12. K. Arrow, "Toward a Theory of Price Adjustments," in M. Abramovitz, ed., *The Allocation of Economic Resources* (Stanford University Press, 1959); and Leijonhufbud, *On Keynesian Economics.*

In such an environment, producers will behave in a very cautious way as regards price changes. They will set up simple markup rules so that cost increases are passed on to prices in a predictable way. On the other hand, if demand changes, they will adjust prices slowly. If demand falls, they will not reduce prices for fear of not gaining a larger share of the market. They will act in this cautious manner until they can get enough information so that the risk of profit losses due to wrong price decisions is minimized.

Most of the effect we have described is transitory and will last as long as the disequilibrium state persists. But there is one factor that would permanently affect the speed of price adjustment: this is the existence of oligopolistic structures as such. This seems to be the case for large segments of the modern manufacturing sector in semi-industrialized economies, like the ones we have been dealing with. The prevalence of oligopoly will only reinforce the tendency for slow price adjustment in the economy vis-à-vis changes in demand.

All this adds up to the following. When the drastic relative price changes brought about by the stabilization policy disequilibrium prevails and demand falls sharply, it is quite likely that the economy will adjust mainly by reducing output and employment levels first, and only then and gradually, by reducing the rate of increase in prices.[13] The lower income levels and higher unemployment that result from this type of adjustment negatively affects income distribution.

Deregulation of Financial Markets

Deregulating financial markets is another aspect of the policies oriented to correct relative prices (negative real interest rates prevailed when interest rates were regulated)

13. The behavior of this type of economy, under disequilibrium, would probably be closer to the fixed-price models of Barro and Grossman, Lei-

and to stimulate private sector savings and investment (part of the long-term neoconservative project).

Let us examine here the development of private financial markets and the effects this policy action may have when undertaken simultaneously with a policy of monetary restraint. Let us suppose that while monetary contraction is underway and recession is setting in, private financial intermediaries are created and the previously controlled interest rate is allowed to fluctuate freely according to supply and demand conditions.

This is what happened in Chile during 1974 when private financiers were allowed to operate under a system of free interest rates. At the same time, the rate charged by banks was under control of the monetary authorities. Typically, the former was about 50% higher than the latter.[14] In April 1975, bank rates were set free. They jumped by more than 100% in nominal terms during the first quarter of 1975, as can be seen in Figure 5.

A similar behavior is observed in Argentina. A financial reform program was implemented in May 1977 when banks were allowed to operate in the short-term financial market with free interest rates.[15] At the same time, the demand for

---

jonhufbud, Malinvaud, and Muellbauer and Portes than that predicted by the competitive model with auction markets à la Walras. Employment would be more sensitive to expected demand than to wage levels. A decrease in real wages would have a contractionary effect in demand and, through the Keynesian multiplier, in output and employment. Real income effects would be important during the adjustment process, giving rise to marked income distribution changes. See R. Barro and H. Grossman, "A General Disequilibrium Model of Income and Employment," *American Economic Review,* March 1971; Leijonhufbud, *On Keynesian Economics;* E. Malinvaud, *The Theory of Unemployment Reconsidered* (Halsted Press, 1977); Muellbauer and Portes, "Macroeconomic Models."

14. Average normal monthly rates for the first three months in 1975 charged by financiers was 14.3% as compared with 9.6% charged by banks.

15. See A. Canitrot and R. Frenkel, "Estabilización y largo plazo: La experiencia argentina 1976–1979," CEDES (mimeo), Buenos Aires, June 1979.

funds by public enterprises was channeled to this market. The effect was that nominal monthly interest rates rose from 6% in May to 13% by the end of the year, graph (1) in Figure 4, where the equivalent rates for ninety days are given.

The effect of such a sharp rise in interest rates is equivalent to a supply shock. The cost of financial capital for firms rises, and this will eventually have an effect on prices. Empirical evidence that this effect might be important in the context of semi-industrialized countries has been provided by Cavallo.[16]

An explanation of why the cost of borrowing may be an important factor in the pricing behavior of firms, and the macroeconomic implications of it, are developed by Cavallo and more recently by Bruno.[17] The story runs as follows. Conventional macrotheory has emphasized wages as the main cost-push factor behind price determination by firms in the short run. The underlying assumption is that capital is constant and that raw materials prices do not change significantly throughout the cycle. The assumption seems to be justified with respect to physical capital but not necessarily about working capital, which is not a fixed cost. It is, in fact, a function of the funds required to finance labor and physical inputs and of the interest rate.

If for some reason the demand for funds increases or the supply is rationed and interest rates rise sharply, there will be a cost-push effect on firms. A higher cost of borrowing shifts aggregate supply upward. How important will this effect be? It will depend on the relative importance of the rise in interest rates. Ordinarily, in economies with developed, homogeneous

16. D. Cavallo, Stagflationary Effects of Monetarist Stabilization Policies in Economies with Persistent Inflation," Ph.D. diss., Harvard University, 1977.

17. M. Bruno, "Stabilization and Stagflation in a Semi-Industrialized Economy," in R. Dornbusch and J. A. Frenkel, eds., *International Economic Policy: Theory and Evidence* (Johns Hopkins University Press, 1979).

capital markets, these changes are not large, even in the face of a restrictive monetary policy.[18]

The same cannot be said for semi-industrialized economies with segmented financial markets. Here a restrictive monetary policy may have a very sharp effect on the cost of borrowing. This may force firms out of the official low interest rate market into the high-cost financial market.[19] In fact, the higher credit supply is and the more segmented the financial market, the more significant cost effect will be.

What kind of financial market segmentation were these economies facing? As has already been stated, during a first phase the market was segmented between an official regulated market (the banking system) and a higher cost, free market (the financiers). Both were essentially domestic markets. During a second phase, domestic interest rates were set free. The official and private domestic markets became one, with one interest rate charged. The interest rate, now determined by supply and demand conditions, rapidly reached a much higher level than the official rate. This had a cost-push effect on firms. At the same time, external borrowing became more attractive. The cost of borrowing abroad, for those banks and firms that had access to foreign capital markets, was substantially lower than the domestic cost.[20] Since there were regulations concerning the maximum volume of borrowing allowed, the external financial market acted as a rationed, cheap credit market for those firms that had access to it. Thus, a second kind of market segmentation was established, this time between the free domestic market and the cheap, rationed external market.

18. J. Tobin, "Inflation and Unemployment," *American Economic Review,* March 1972.

19. For example, borrowing from banks at the official rate during 1974 in Chile may not have been possible for many firms due to the contractionary monetary policy. They were then forced to borrow, at a cost higher by 50%, from the financiers.

20. In the Chilean case, for a sustained period of time, the external cost of borrowing was between one-fourth and one-half the internal cost.

FIGURE 4
Argentina: Selected Indicators
(quarterly variations and index)

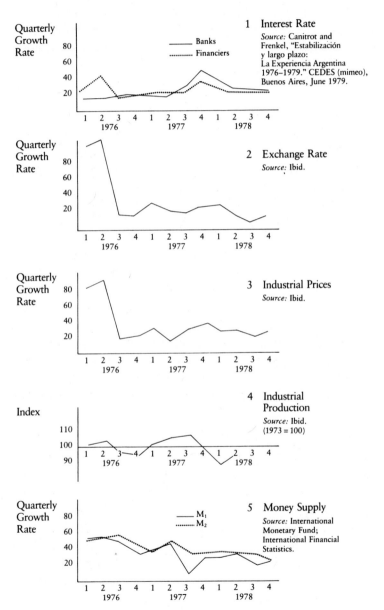

FIGURE 5
Chile: Selected Indicators
(quarterly variations and index)

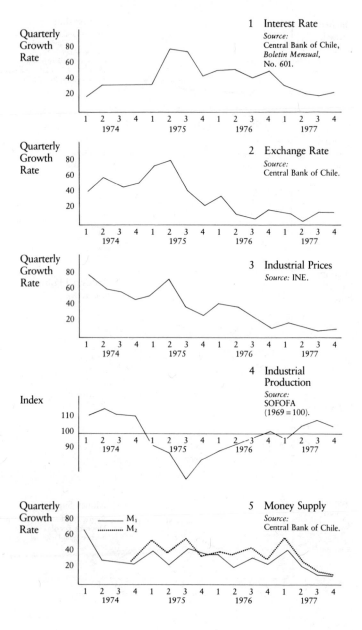

For firms facing the expensive domestic financial market, the situation is difficult not only because of cost pressures due to high interest rates. At the same time, demand is falling due to the restrictive monetary policy. The higher cost of credit and demand restrictions forces them to reduce stocks. They do this by diminishing production. The effect of the higher financial cost is not only to increase prices but also to reduce output, a typical stagflationary effect.[21] The trends shown by the variables in Figures 4 and 5 seem to be consistent with this hypothesis.

The effect will be temporary and may, thus, be considered unimportant.[22] But given that it tends to happen simultaneously with other macro adjustments, like devaluation and monetary contraction, it tends to reinforce the stagflationary effects produced by some of these other mechanisms. On the other hand, given that the economy is facing a very high rate of inflation for a sustained period, inflationary expectations perform an important amplifying role vis-à-vis any changes in such critical indicators as the exchange rate, wages, and the interest rate. This is a powerful reason for not underestimating the impact of financial costs on the rate of inflation and the level of economic activity and employment, at least while financial market segmentation is a significant structural characteristic of the economy.

A "side-effect" of this policy has to do with important processes of asset redistribution that are facilitated by a macroeconomic environment, such as the one we have been describing in this section. The prevalence of high real interest rates—in Chile

21. Notice that the stagflationary effects occur simultaneously with a general policy of monetary contraction. And at least during the period when the financial supply shock is absorbed, what is observed is not a reduction in output and rates of inflation but lower output with higher inflation, a "perverse" result according to conventional theory.

22. The rise in domestic interest rates could be very temporary if, simultaneous with setting it free, external capital were allowed to move in with no restrictions.

they were over 40% a year for about three years—implies huge distortions that affect resource allocation.[23] Resources do not flow into new real investment unless rates of return similar to those prevailing in the financial markets can be obtained elsewhere. This can only occur if the price of productive assets drastically goes down.

On the other hand, not all firms are equally affected by monetary contraction. Large firms are able rapidly to develop an access to foreign borrowing. Since the external rates are equivalent to one-half or a third of that prevailing in the domestic markets, this gives large firms a significant advantage. Thus, liquidity concentrates in larger firms. It is easy for them, under those conditions, to buy "undervalued" assets of medium-size firms that are in trouble because of low sales and increased borrowing at the very high rates prevailing in the domestic market.

Again, the mechanism we have described is not merely an abstract exercise. At least in the Chilean case, it has proved to be a very powerful mechanism for concentrating assets in few large conglomerates.[24] The process is accelerated if it coincides with the privatization of public enterprises, a common objective of the "new" orthodox stabilization policies in Latin America. Undervalued public enterprises will be transferred at low prices and bought by those very few who have access to liquid funds in favorable conditions.[25]

In sum, the persistence of financial market segmentation, together with general recessionary conditions in the economy,

23. Notice that the interest rates given in Figures 1 and 2 are nominal quarterly rates. They are consistent with the yearly real rates.
24. In 1978 five economic groups in Chile controlled companies whose assets represented more than 50% of the 250 largest private enterprises. Nine conglomerates, including those five, controlled 82% of bank assets.
25. Again an example from Chile is illustrative. Of 121 public firms that were sold to the private sector between 1975 and 1977 for $290 million, the assets of only twenty-one of these were valued at $301 million in 1977, according to their balance sheets; see Foxley, "Stabilization Policies and Stagflation."

has two kinds of effects. It sets in motion a powerful process of asset concentration. On the other hand, it generates stagflation. Both effects have a negative impact on the distribution of income.

External Shocks and Devaluation

Exchange rate devaluation is a third policy action in the area of corrections to inherited relative price distortions. In fact, chronic balance of payments disequilibrium has been a structural feature of most Latin American economies for decades. These imbalances have been aggravated by external supply shocks—autonomous price increases in imported raw materials—that became a part of the scene in the 1970s. This is the reason for the drastic and recurrent devaluations that have gone together with monetary control, wage repression, and the other policies that form part of the initial orthodox package, in the cases that we have been analyzing.

Let us take the cases of Chile and Argentina as an illustration. A look at Figures 4 and 5 indicates the various instances in which a devaluation of the peso was taking place. In Chile, starting in November 1974 and during the first semester of 1975, the peso was devalued at a faster rate than during the first ten months in 1974.[26] This process was accompanied by an upsurge in prices.[27] Similar but even more discontinuous devaluations took place in Argentina in the first and last quarters of 1976 and again in the fourth quarter of 1977. These were also accompanied by price increases, as is suggested by Figure 4.

26. Average devaluation during the first nine months was 43% per quarter. The last quarter of 1974 was 58.5%, and it went up to 71.9% and 64.3% in the first and second quarters of 1975.

27. Although average price increases for the period Oct.–Dec. 1974 were 41% between Jan. and March 1975, the rate of inflation went up to 60%, and in the second quarter, the inflation rate for the three-month period increased to 73.7%.

What are the effects of devaluations on semi-industrialized economies like the ones we have examined? Conventional theory predicts that devaluation, by improving the relative price of traded vis-à-vis nontraded goods, shifts resources toward export or import substituting activities, thus helping reduce the balance of payments deficit. At the same time, an excess demand for the relatively cheaper nontraded goods develops. This results either in a price increase of domestic goods if the economy is in full employment or in an expansion of nontraded goods production. Introducing money and capital flows in the analysis does not change the basic conclusions.[28]

This approach overlooks some important effects that might go together with the change in relative prices, resulting from exogenous changes in import prices or from devaluation. One is a probable strong and immediate impact on inflationary expectations, particularly when the economy is suffering from very high inflation rates.[29] Another less conventional impact of devaluation may be that of generating a contractionary effect on effective demand and income, of a more permanent nature than the one predicted by conventional theory.

Suppose nominal wages are constant or only partially indexed with respect to the rate of inflation. When the price of traded goods increases as a result of devaluation, there follows a cost increase for firms because the price of imported inputs

28. Essentially, a real cash balances effect reduces income, thus depressing imports until a surplus in current accounts is developed. This very short-run effect is accompanied by a flow of foreign capital, given that the original trade deficit creates an excess demand for money. Interest rates rise and capital flows in, helping cover the deficit and expanding money supply; see R. Dornbusch, "Real and Monetary Aspects of the Effects of Exchange Rate Changes," in R. Z. Aliber, ed., *National Monetary Policies and the International Financial System* (University of Chicago Press, 1974). See also L. Calmfors, *Prices, Wages, and Employment in the Open Economy* (Institute for International Economic Studies, University of Stockholm, 1978).

29. L. Sjaastad and H. Cortés find evidence of this in the Chilean case; see their "El enfoque monetario de la balanza de pagos y las tasas de interés real en Chile," *Estudios de Economía*, No. 11, University of Chile, 1st semester, 1978.

raises. Some of the cost pressure is transferred to domestic prices through a markup mechanism. Now the prices of traded and nontraded goods are rising, but nominal wages do not keep up with the price increase caused by devaluation.

Real wages and the wage share fall. Income distribution shifts toward profit earners—exporters particularly—and the government via increased export and import tax revenues. It suffices that the saving propensities of the latter two will be higher than those of wage earners for the net effect on aggregate demand to be contractionary. Savings will be in excess of required levels, and the economy will adjust by reducing income. The impact of devaluation will be recessionary.[30]

The same type of result will be obtained if it is assumed that devaluation acts over a large and chronic balance of payments deficit. In this case, even if the trade balance improves in terms of foreign currency after devaluation, it may actually result in a larger deficit in domestic currency.[31] This is because the price increase brought about by devaluation raises spending for imports in domestic currency more than it increases export revenues. If money supply is endogenous and directly dependent on the trade balance in domestic currency, nominal money balances will fall as a consequence. Since at the same time prices are rising, real balances fall even more and the final effect is recessionary.

These results are dependent on some key assumptions. One, explicit both in the Taylor and Bruno approaches, is that the price elasticities involved (demand for imports, supply of exports) are small. In other words, they share a pessimism about the capacity of the economy to respond quickly to devaluation

30. This approach has been developed in an interesting article by P. Krugman and L. Taylor, "Contractionary Effects of Devaluation," *Journal of International Economics,* No. 8, 1978; see also L. Taylor, *Macro Models for Developing Countries* (McGraw-Hill, 1979).
31. A model along these lines was proposed by Bruno, "Stabilization and Stagflation."

through higher exports and lower imports. In effect, Krugman and Taylor's argument is that income distribution effects will reduce aggregate demand (absorption) and that this reduction will dominate any improvement that might be achieved in the trade balance. This is the only way that the net effect is recessionary.

But recent experience, including countries like Uruguay, Brazil, and Chile, seems to suggest that export pessimism does not seem to be warranted, given the success of these countries in expanding nontraditional exports when the exchange rate bias against exports is eliminated. This is in agreement with empirical studies for a large number of countries.[32]

If this is so, the impact of devaluation could go either way. It would be recessionary only if—in spite of significant improvements in the trade balance—the depressive effect of devaluation on internal demand is very strong and dominant. This seems to be the case in Argentina where the basic traded exportables are food products that represent a large share of domestic consumption. Thus, devaluation has a very large and direct impact through higher prices of traded consumption goods and lower real wages on real domestic consumption. This generates an almost immediate recessionary tendency. This relationship is certainly suggested in Figure 4 and has been demonstrated at the theoretical and empirical level in several studies.[33]

Another important premise in the previous analysis is that international capital flows are controlled by the government, for if this were not the case, the recessionary tendency would be checked because any reduction in real monetary balances caused by the price increases that follow devaluation would be

32. See J. Bhagwati and R. Martin, "Trade and Investment Strategies, Jobs, and Poverty," MIT (mimeo), Aug. 1979.

33. The pioneering work was done by C. Díaz-Alejandro, *Exchange Rate Devaluation in a Semi-Industrialized Country: The Experience of Argentina* (MIT Press, 1965).

compensated for by a higher inflow of external capital. This would expand the money supply.[34] Under these conditions, there need not be a recession as a consequence of devaluing the domestic currency.

On the other hand, when these conditions are not met, as is often the case in most semi-industrialized economies (particularly relative to free capital movements), the likelihood of recession following devaluation increases. And a direct impact on prices—both through higher costs and inflationary expectations—is almost a certainty.[35] Neither of these effects helps improve income distribution particularly when nominal wages are fixed or only partially indexed.

Adjustment Mechanism in the Open Economy: Tariff Reduction as a Stabilization Instrument

An important part of orthodox stabilization is the opening up of the economy to free trade and capital flows. In this section we will examine the role of external price competition—through lower trade barriers—as a stabilization instrument whereas in the next section we will discuss capital flows liberalization. A component of orthodox stabilization in Latin America has been the opening up of the economy to foreign competition by gradually lowering tariffs. It has been hoped that when external tariffs have been sufficiently reduced, those sectors in the domestic economy that produce in-

34. See Sjaastad and Cortés, "El enfoque monetario"; see also A. Harberger, "Una visión moderna del fenómeno inflacionario," in *Cuadernos de Economía,* Catholic University of Chile, Dec. 1977.

35. Unless the effect of devaluation is compensated for by tariff reductions; but, in that case, an important expected result of the policy, that of checking import expansion by increasing its relative price, is canceled.

ternationally traded goods will be subject to a price ceiling given by external prices, assuming tariffs are sufficiently low and the exchange rate is fixed. If tariffs and the exchange rate are fixed and markets are transparent, the evolution of international prices should dictate the rate of increase of domestic prices, at least in that part of the economy that is exposed to foreign competition.

But even before that point near free trade has been reached, lower tariffs may have an effect on domestic prices, provided the cost of imports goes down significantly. This is a function not only of tariff reduction but of the exchange rate as well. In the case of Argentina, tariff reduction was not significant during the first three critical years of the stabilization program. Starting from an average nominal rate of 55% for 1976, no effective reductions were undertaken until the end of 1978[36] and very gradually with a 15% target average tariff for 1984. On the other hand, between 1976 and 1978 the real exchange rate stayed constant.[37] Thus, the cost of imports was not significantly altered. In Uruguay the situation was similar. Tariff reductions did not start until 1978, the fifth year in the stabilization program, and the real value of the exchange rate was maintained constant between 1974 and 1978.[38]

It is only in the Chilean case that the opening up to trade may have had an effect on the stabilization process, although not until the third year (1976). On the one hand, tariff reductions were more drastic. Average nominal tariffs were reduced

36. See A. Ferrer, "Política económica comparada: El monetarismo en Argentina y Chile," IDES (mimeo), Buenos Aires, June 1980; and M. Rimez, "Las experiencias de apertura externa y desprotección industrial," in *Economía de América Latina*, CIDE, México, March 1979.

37. R. Frenkel, "La apertura financiera externa: El caso argentino," paper presented to the Conference on International Financial Markets and Their Impact on Latin America, CIEPLAN, Santiago, March 1981.

38. Rimez, "Las experiencias de apertura externa"; and CINVE, *Un nuevo ensayo de reajuste económico: Uruguay 1974–1979*, Documento de Trabajo, CINVE, Montevideo, 1980.

from 94% in 1973 to 10% in 1979. And the real exchange rate deteriorated from mid-1976 until the end of 1977, staying constant thereafter until mid-1979. As a consequence, the cost of imports fell as much as 42% between the last quarter of 1975 and the end of the last quarter of 1977, staying constant afterwards until June 1979 when the fixed exchange rate policy was established.[39] Cheaper imports contributed to moderating the rate of increase in domestic prices of tradable goods.

What are the perspectives for a policy of low tariffs to perform a stabilizing role over domestic prices? Let us examine a theoretical situation first. In a pure case where all or most of domestic production is internationally traded and the exchange rate is fixed, the domestic rate of inflation would be fully determined by world inflation, after account is taken for the required adjustment lags and convergence processes. In this environment, monetary policy would not play any significant role in the stabilization strategy. If prices are fully flexible and the economy is in full employment equilibrium, a tight money policy would result in a transitory lower level of domestic prices vis-à-vis external prices. This would stimulate exports and reduce the demand for imports, with a subsequent accumulation of reserves that expands the monetary base, putting an upward pressure on domestic prices until the balance of payments surplus disappears and full employment equilibrium is restored. Adjustment is automatic, and there is no need for an elaborate stabilization program.

Obviously, there are many departures from the ideal world described above. The economy does not usually exhibit fully flexible prices and full employment, as argued in earlier sections in this chapter. The internationally traded goods sector in an economy is only a fraction of the total, typically between a

39. These figures have been taken from R. Ffrench-Davis, "Liberalización de importaciones: La experiencia chilena en 1973–1979," *Colección Estudios CIEPLAN*, No. 4, 1980.

third and one-half of the domestic productive structure. On the other hand, market imperfections abound in the traded goods sector: product differentiation allows producers to charge prices above international prices or importers to charge higher markups than those consistent with normal profits in a competitive environment. All these imperfections make for a slow convergence process between international and domestic prices, as empirical studies show.[40] On the other hand, the non-traded goods sector may be an autonomous source of inflationary pressures. Prices in this sector are not governed by international prices but by domestic supply and demand conditions.

Thus, it seems that in the real world and during the transition period in which the economy is simultaneously attempting to stabilize the price level and gradually reduce tariffs, the role of tariff reduction in the stabilization effort is limited. The key elements for the success or failure of the stabilization program still lie in domestic economic forces and processes.

Adjustment Mechanisms in the Open Economy: The Role of External Capital Flows

Liberalization of external capital flows is the other element in a policy of opening up the economy to world markets. Latin America pursued a vigorous liberalization policy in order to attract foreign capital. This process was facilitated by the fact that international liquidity was high after the oil crisis and that private lending institutions were more than willing to lend in countries where economic orthodoxy seemed to constitute the best safeguard against risky investments. The

40. W. Nordhaus, "Inflation Theory and Policy," *American Economic Review,* May 1976.

elimination of restrictions to foreign borrowing was gradual but steady in the cases of Argentina, Chile, and Uruguay.

The sudden access to a rapidly growing international private financial market, while opening up possibilities, also created new problems in the management of the economies and particularly in the implementation of the stabilization policies. It created distortions in various spheres, including the managing of monetary and exchange rate policies, as will be illustrated below.

Monetary policy was one of the areas where deregulation of capital flows posed serious difficulties. Let us illustrate the problem with the cases of Chile and Argentina. As early as 1976 in Chile and 1977 in Argentina, the accumulation of reserves was the main factor in the creation of high-powered money.[41] Had the economy been fully open, including trade flows, the problems would not have been so serious, given the larger degree of automaticity in the adjustment process, as predicted by the monetary approach to the balance of payments. Alternatively, a closed economy setting required that effective ways of sterilizing money creation generated in the external sector be developed so that the monetary authority would maintain control of the key policy instrument, the rate of expansion in money supply.

As it happened, the economy was usually in an intermediate situation: a transition from a closed to an open economy. Under these conditions, capital inflows expanded money supply. Monetary authorities reacted by reducing domestic credit expansion or by curtailing government expenditures beyond the original targets, given the need to keep overall monetary growth within the limits required by the stabilization program. If private credit was reduced beyond the initial already contrac-

41. See Frenkel, "La apertura financiera externa"; and R. Ffrench-Davis and J.P. Arellano, "Apertura financiera externa: La experiencia chilena en 1973–1980," *Colección Estudios CIEPLAN*, No. 5, 1981.

tionary levels, excess demand for credit would push interest rates up, inducing higher prices and output reductions, the typical stagflationary effect of monetary contraction under imperfect financial intermediation, as discussed earlier. The process was repeatedly observed in Chile and particularly in Argentina during recent stabilization attempts.

One way out of the problem was to abandon monetary contraction as a target and let external capital flow in; then domestic interest rates would go down and no stagflationary effects would follow. Of course, because of money creation, domestic inflation would not go down as fast as desired.

Another consequence of money expansion through reserve accumulation was that fiscal policy had to be even more severe than it would have been in another context. Government expenditures had to be reduced to the point not only of eliminating the deficit but hopefully creating a fiscal surplus that would compensate for the unduly large expansionary money-creation effect of external capital flows. Severe budget cuts can be implemented, but the more severe they are, the more they will affect social programs, one of the few elements in a stabilization package that can be used effectively to compensate lower-income groups from losses suffered elsewhere. Thus, the regressive impact of the policy package was probably enhanced because of this factor. The regressive impact is greatest when some large components of public expenditures, like defense, cannot be cut and are in fact rapidly growing. Chilean fiscal policy in 1975 followed just this course.[42]

A second area where policy outcomes are affected by external financial liberalization is that of trade policy itself. Exchange rate devaluation will usually improve the trade balance but will decrease capital inflows to the extent that present devaluation reinforces expectations of future devaluations. On

42. R Zahler, "Repercusiones monetarias y reales de la apertura de la economía chilena 1975 –1978," *Revista de la CEPAL,* April 1980.

the other hand, a revaluation will produce the opposite effect: it will worsen the trade balance by making imports cheaper and discouraging exports. At the same time, it will make capital inflows more attractive since the effective interest rate paid to foreign lenders will be the domestic rate plus the expected rate of revaluation.[43] These effects may be cumulative. Assume that high domestic interest rates induce a capital inflow, and this results in revaluation. As long as foreign lenders expect that the monetary authority will react by revaluing domestic currency every time a surplus occurs in the balance of payments, an additional inflow of capital will be likely after the first revaluation. This was the reaction in Chile after the first revaluation in June 1976.

This kind of effect will be reinforced if a deindexation program for the exchange rate is announced for several months, as was done in Argentina by the end of 1978.[44] Now the capital inflow will be much larger. Money supply will increase sharply, domestic inflation will go up, and, as a consequence, the real exchange rate will lag behind. The process may not be convergent. Higher capital account surpluses are accompanied by ever higher current account deficits and overvalued domestic currency. At one point expectations reverse themselves. As domestic inflation continues to be substantially higher than external inflation and trade deficits increase, the credibility of the policy of deindexing the exchange rate weakens. Capital inflows will diminish. When the expectations of a devaluation are high, flows will rapidly change sign and a massive capital outflow is possible.

Then the economy is in the worst of both worlds: it has a huge current account deficit and experiences loss of reserves at

43. These mechanisms are described in R. McKinnon, "Intermediación financiera y control monetario en Chile," *Cuadernos de Economía*, Dec. 1977.
   44. See Frenkel, "La apertura financiera externa," for a full development of the arguments and description of events in the Argentine case.

a time when inflation is still high and production lagging. The exchange rate policy has led to misallocation of resources by penalizing exports and still has not accomplished the purpose of continuously attracting foreign capital and checking inflation. The economy faces the possibility of a sharp rise in interest rates if the loss of reserves is not compensated by money creation elsewhere. On the other hand, foreign exchange devaluation is unavoidable. The combination of both measures will certainly accelerate inflation again and will start a new recessionary cycle.

Events in Argentina after 1980 followed precisely this pattern. After a period of deindexation of the exchange rate initiated in May 1978 that led to a net inflow of capital of over $4 billion in 1979, resilient domestic inflation (around 100% a year), plus deficits in the current account close to $1 billion as of the last quarter in 1979, led to a drastic change in expectations that resulted in capital flight. Loss of reserves reached $1.5 billion in the second quarter of 1980 alone.

Distortions such as those mentioned in this section are dependent not only on the degree to which the economy is opened up but also on the timing of the policies. If trade restrictions are eliminated without changes in the financial side, that will imply that the opening up process will be accompanied by larger devaluations than would be necessary had capital movements been freed. This will certainly induce higher exports but will also have a negative effect on costs and inflationary expectations. It is likely to lead to a cost-push, expectations-reinforced inflation.

The opposite course, which is to liberalize financial flows first, will accumulate reserves and lead to monetary expansion and excess-demand inflation unless reserve creation is sterilized. International prices will not be used as a check for domestic inflation since tariffs have not been reduced. A revalued exchange rate will help curb cost pressures and expectations for the time being. At the same time, it will certainly cause resource misallocation, which will manifest itself in a smaller traded-goods sector in the economy, a result opposite to what policy-makers would expect from the opening up policy.

The relative importance of each of these effects depends on a multitude of factors, such as the relative importance of the initial disequilibrium, the nature of the inflationary process, supply and demand elasticities in the traded goods sector, etc. The optimal path will be influenced as much by the value of these parameters as by the objectives that are being pursued: how much inflation and recession is tolerable and for how long during the stabilization process, what pattern of resource allocation, distribution of income, and assets is desired, and what form of integration with world markets is considered optimal. Whatever the final outcome, it is clear that the financial opening in the context of excess liquidity in international financial markets was bound to create a whole set of new problems to stabilization attempts in the Latin American economies in the 1970s and 1980s.

8

Common Themes

IT is now time to consider some of the common themes that have emerged in our attempt to evaluate current neoconservative economic policies in Latin America. As it is clear from our study, it would make little sense to undertake this task *solely* by a piecemeal approach, that is, by evaluating each policy instrument independently and on its own merits, as some conventional economists would argue.

This conventional approach is valid and useful, but insufficient. As we have argued, the neoconservative experiment in Latin America often represents a complete turnaround with respect to previous policies, not only marginal changes. The experiment involves systemic changes, not only adjustment processes. Correctly understanding the dimensions of the phenomena is of the essence in order to do meaningful social science and to reach relevant conclusions. This effort includes but goes well beyond the examination of specific policy instruments.

The Neoconservative Program

The final objective of neoconservatism in Latin America is nothing less than radically transforming the way the economy operates and, in its more radical version, the way society and political institutions are organized. The attempt to achieve these objectives may work or fail, but it is always subjacent in the neoconservative agenda. Whether it succeeds or fails will depend on a number of factors, among them the strength of the military and the ruling coalition vis-à-vis civil society, the effectiveness of the initial corrective economic measures, the availability of abundant external capital, and even sheer luck.

But it must again be stressed that analyzing neoconservative policies in Latin America means studying social and economic phenomena that go well beyond IMF-type stabilization policies. On the one hand, at least partly out of a profound dislike by neoconservatives of the old reformist, populist economic system, their diagnosis of such economic ills as inflation and balance of payments deficits tends to turn into a structural argument. If the problem is structural, then its solution must be radical and global: inflation will not go away unless the whole way the economy functions is changed. As Hirschman has pointed out, we have become used to hearing this argument as part of the critique from the Left. It is interesting to notice that it is now very much at the core of the neoconservative position as well, although obviously the nature of the structural changes advocated by both groups are at opposite extremes.

This radicalization of neoconservative thought in Latin America is related to many factors that we examined in Chapter 2. We will not repeat them here. We would like to stress only that, as a result, a drastic change in development strategy, in the role assigned to various economic agents, and in the power structure follows. The Chilean case, discussed in Chapters 3 and 4, is perhaps a clear-cut case of profound changes in these various dimensions. The observed concentration of assets and income was very much conditioned by the nature of changes in the power structure in Chile and not solely because of the economic instruments used. The nonneutral utilization of stabilization instruments (favoring capital owners at the expense of other groups) was to a large extent a consequence of those changes in the political sphere.

A radical conservative economic program has costs. Only part of these costs originate in inadequate stabilization policies. Another important part originates in the need that radical conservatives feel to push simultaneously for structural-institutional changes and macroeconomic adjustment policies. Policy consistency is made much more difficult because of this urge to proceed simultaneously on all fronts. As a consequence, the initial, more restricted aim of the policies—economic stabilization—is postponed. The adjustment process turns out to be longer than expected and more painful in terms of its social cost. Unemployment reaches a higher level and stays there for a longer period of time, wages lag behind prices, and income distribution deteriorates well beyond ex ante expectations.

All these problems can be handled if the authoritarian regime is able to suppress political opposition and discontent. Unexpected help may come from the international financial community. Private banks abroad may look with sympathy on the turn toward economic orthodoxy. When domestic interest rates are so much higher than international ones, that sympathy is reinforced by a high, quick rate of return on the loans. The critical importance of this factor cannot be stressed enough in the Latin American cases that we have examined. Little of what was achieved could have been obtained were it not for the abundant supply of cheap external loans. They proved to be essential during the adjustment process. They could be used flexibly so that more severe disruptions (bankruptcies, higher unemployment) could be avoided. In a way, this new "fortuitous" factor emerging in the 1970s made the experiments possible. Similar radical experiments in turning the economy around in such a short period of time probably would not have worked in the international economic environment of the 1960s with its tied official loans and scarce private credit.

The degree of success in neoconservative experiments in

Latin America varies widely. Of recent cases in Latin America, Chile looked the most successful up until 1980, but the economy entered into a severe crisis in 1981. Argentina was a total failure, and Uruguay is somewhat in between. An examination of the Argentine and Chilean cases suggests that there seems to be an achievement threshold that the regimes had to pass before the more serious and radical institutional changes were undertaken. These achievement thresholds refer to the economic stabilization goals in the first place. But they also refer to the ability to carry out such structural changes quickly, such as reducing the size of the state and opening up the economy to foreign trade and financial flows. If significant progress is made in all these fronts, the regime may pursue new, more ambitious objectives, like the seven modernizations and constitutional changes that were undertaken in Chile after 1979. For this to happen, the ruling coalition must remain solidly behind the military government. The latter must show signs of not having lost momentum or vitality for the new ambitious tasks that lie ahead.

The escalation of economic and institutional objectives is fed not only by relative success in the previous phases. It is also greatly helped by a process of ideology formulation and adaptation. Ideology must not be considered as a remote, abstract construction in the context of revolutionary changes, as the ones discussed in this book. Ideology suffers continuous modifications during the process of changes in the economic and power structure. Ideology must orient those changes, but it must adapt to them as well if it is to remain a cohesive element behind the dissimilar interests of the various groups that participate in the neoconservative experiment. Official ideology must conform, to some extent, to actual processes and make them intelligible in the light of noble, elevated ideals that will lead society to a more perfect stage. This role of ideology, discussed in Chapter 4, should not be underestimated in its importance as a force articulating interests and keeping the faith of the faithful alive throughout the various difficult phases that the experiment must pass in order to be successful.

Policy Performance

All of Part 2 of this book was devoted to the analysis of monetarist stabilization policies that constitute a central component of the neoconservative program. In trying to answer why the stabilization policies generated a long stagflation, our evaluation stressed those aspects of the policies that did not work adequately. But this should not lead us to underestimate the achievements, however partial they might have been. After all, the rate of inflation was significantly reduced in Chile and (although temporarily) in Uruguay (but very little in Argentina). Exports grew very rapidly in all three cases, and the balance of payments developed a surplus in a rather short period of time (although this was to be a short-lived success in Argentina).

On the other hand, at least in comparative terms with the previous situation, the turn toward economic orthodoxy did imply doing away with many inefficiencies, particularly within the public sector. The restoration of market mechanisms, after the adjustment process was over, made it possible to make economic decisions based on better information than when markets were so disrupted that generalized scarcity and informal rationing were prevalent. At the same time, the economy showed a capacity to adapt and respond to new conditions, particularly price incentives, beyond what most structuralists would have made us believe. This is particularly true of the supply response in exports, given an adequate exchange rate policy. To a lesser extent, it is also true of several branches in the manufacturing sector that seem to have adapted with flexibility to the new external competition arising from tarriff reductions.

This is not to say that policy performance, in balance, was impressive. In fact, there are many grounds on which the policies cannot be considered successful, and we have illustrated these. Let us take three important issues: policy consistency, policy efficiency, and neutrality.

Policy Consistency

The view that emerges from our study is mixed. On the one hand, policy consistency in the narrow sense of moving toward fiscal balance and slower expansion in money supply is found at least in one of the cases (Chile) and during some periods in Argentina. But except for the tendencies in fiscal and monetary policies, the stabilization program as a whole does not show a high degree of consistency through time. What we find instead is a zigzagging path where different policy approaches are tried within a general orthodox framework, as was illustrated in Chapters 3 and 5 when discussing the Chilean and Argentine cases.

We identified four different phases in the Chilean stabilization program: a first phase characterized by market deregulation and gradual contractionary policies; a second phase of shock policies consisting of an abrupt reduction in aggregate demand; a third stage in which policies evolved from exclusively demand-centered policies toward an attempt to curb inflationary expectations by manipulating the exchange rate and private credit expansion; and, finally, a stage in which price stabilization was supposed to be achieved by the free play of market forces in the context of an open economy.

Although some of these changes were dictated by disappointing performance, like the shock policies of 1975 in Chile, others were imposed by changing conditions, mainly the degree of opening up of the economy to trade and financial flows. In the Argentinian case, changes were more frequent and closely related to unsatisfactory results. Similar phases of market deregulation, monetary contraction deindexation of critical prices, and global monetarist stabilization were attempted. All of these performed inadequately and led to the next approach to be tried. What this amounts to is a not particularly consistent trial-and-error adjustment process that maintains the economy and disequilibrium for a long period of time and where fluctuations are far from normal or optimal.

The Efficiency Claim

Economic orthodoxy in Latin America has borrowed from monetarism the conviction that inflation "is always and everywhere a monetary phenomenon," hence, the policy conclusion that monetary management is the essential component of successful economic stabilization. What does the Latin American experience show in terms of the efficiency with which this policy was implemented? The record shows that in spite of almost continuous attempts at monetary control, the results were rather poor. Money supply figures do show a general contractionary trend but one that is characterized by wide fluctuations and discontinuities. At least from the point of view of this key policy instrument, efficiency was not impressive. In fact, monetary control proved much more difficult to implement in practice in spite of "favorable" political conditions. Under an authoritarian political climate, pressure groups could not force policymakers to change a contractionist monetary policy. It was the policymakers themselves who failed in carrying out such a key component of the stabilization program.

The conditioning factors were of a varied nature. Price fluctuations for key primary exports like copper, beef, or coffee had a direct repercussion on the trade balance and indirectly generated unexpected fluctuations in money supply. External shocks, like the oil crisis, had a similar effect, altering the monetary program. Other factors were policy-created. Thus, the development of private financial instruments not subject to the same controls as currency and bank deposits had the effect of providing close substitutes for money at a time when the effort was concentrated on controlling one particular monetary aggregate, that is, currency and demand deposits in the banking system. Since the incentives operated in the direction of the substitutes, more and more money creation took place away from the control of the monetary authority, making monetary management all the more difficult.

On the other hand, an early overkill in the reduction of aggregate demand, illustrated in Chapters 6 and 7, also made sustained money supply contraction more difficult. With real wages going down by 40%, unemployment up to 20%, or public investment being cut in half, the economy was bound to enter into a severe recession. Additional monetary contraction would make things intolerable even for those willing to administer a painful medicine, as the military were. Given these facts, it is likely that a more lenient monetary policy will be the result of such severe stagflation.

Surprises also played a role in making monetary policy less effective than expected. Deregulation of prices, interest rates, and exchange rate devaluations had an unexpected stagflationary effect that reinforced the initial contraction in aggregate demand, as was argued extensively in Chapter 7. Too much recession, too soon, forced some passivity in monetary policy.

But perhaps the most determining factor was the increased endogeneity of money supply as the process of financial liberalization was underway. This proved to be a very difficult problem for the monetary authority. Credit restrictions pushed domestic interest rates up, creating a large differential with the external rate, even when expected devaluation was taken into account. This induced a massive capital inflow that resulted—given recessionary conditions in the economy—in the accumulation of reserves that in turn expanded the monetary base. Both in Chile and Argentina this was the single most important factor behind unprogramed expansions in money supply. In sum, the management of money supply encountered severe problems in spite of policymakers' intentions and noninterference from special interest groups. The money supply was affected by numerous exogenous factors that the monetary authorities could not or did not know how to control.

The results should not have been unexpected after all. A one-equation view of the economy—the notion that the stability of the demand for money guarantees the effectiveness of controlling nominal money supply in the case of the closed economy, or the view that money supply will be automatically regulated through the external sector in the case of global monetarism—rests on the assumption that all other markets are in equilibrium or approaching it. During stabilization, disturbances are likely to be present in the goods, labor, and financial markets. In the end, these will be transferred to the monetary sector as exogenous shocks affecting the equilibrium between supply and demand for money. In the absence of adequate and instantaneous instruments to neutralize the disturbances, money supply is likely to behave in a more unstable and erratic manner than what is intended by well-meaning policymakers.

The Neutrality Issue

It has often been argued that monetarism and free market policies associated with it provide a nondiscretionary, neutral way of restoring equilibrium in the economy. But one of the consistent results in current orthodox programs, illustrated in Chapter 7, was the uniformity in the distributive outcome of the policies: they consistently led to a deterioration in the distribution of income. In cases where empirical evidence was available, it was also shown that assets were more concentrated as a result of the stabilization policies (see Chapter 3).

Income distribution studies usually belong to the realm of the long term. It is widely believed that distributive patterns cannot readily be altered in the short run, given dependency on structural factors. Our conclusions dispute that view. What we have shown is that income and asset distribution can be seriously changed even in the short run provided some conditions are present: when there is no symmetric treatment of prices and wages; when deregulation of prices takes place in conditions of imperfect competition, market segmentation, and unequal access to scarce factors of production; if a deliberate policy of asset distribution is undertaken by the government; and when severe market disequilibrium persists for a long period of time, giving rise to all kinds of speculative flows. We will now elaborate on how these factors influence the distributive outcome.

A general characteristic of the stabilization programs was the deregulation of interest rates and goods prices and the severe control of wages that led to sharp reductions in the purchasing power of salaried workers. General contractionary policies generated a recession, and as a consequence, except where deliberate employment policies were pursued, as in Argentina, unemployment increased substantially. When the stabilization cycle is examined carefully, typically it will be found that at the end of the recession, that is, when output (or GDP) has recuperated initial levels, real wages are still well below the benchmark, and the rate of unemployment has not decreased; in fact, it is probably still well above original rates. This amounts to a deterioration in the functional distribution of income: a lower share for labor, a higher share for capital.

Behind the asymmetric treatment of prices and wages lies the notion that for free market policies to operate efficiently, previous distortions in relative prices must be corrected. The presumption is that labor is overpaid while the price of capital is below its equilibrium value. The question that comes to mind is why does the free market not take care of these distortions without government intervention? It is implicitly assumed within this policy framework that market imperfections are more important in the labor market than in other markets and that collective bargaining, if allowed to operate, would result in higher than optimal payments to labor, reflecting union strength and political clout rather than a free expression of competitive forces. Organized labor has to be disciplined before it is allowed to play the free market game.

Another reason for this discriminatory policy has to do with a deliberate attempt to redress production incentives toward capital. Since so much of the success of the orthodox program is tied to its capacity to accelerate growth, a pro-business bias readily sets in. For higher growth rates to be achieved, capital accumulation has to increase and entrepreneurial innovation must be stimulated. Free prices and reduced real wages play a role here, as well as specific supply-side incentives. Among these are reductions in tax rates for corporations and in property taxes, elimination of taxes on net wealth and capital gains, accelerated depreciation allowances, and other equally generous tax incentives for domestic business firms. At the same time, similar measures are undertaken to make foreign investment more profitable. Obviously, many of these policies reinforce the regressive effect of the package. But this is thought to be unavoidable: some cost must be paid in terms of equity if more growth is to be achieved.

A related set of policies having a serious impact on income distribution is the general movement toward free markets that characterizes monetarist policies. A free market is assumed to set uniform rules for all economic agents. In this sense, it would not discriminate in favor of or against special interest groups, as political decision making would. Of course, this is debatable, first, because markets do not function in a political vacuum and are thus influenced by political forces and events; and, second, because economic power in the market is not equally distributed, nor is the access to scarce resources (credit, foreign exchange, technology, information). This will give an advantage to those having privileged access (usually large firms) vis-à-vis those who do not have such an access.

Unequal market power or unequal access to resources are conditions under which apparently neutral policies produce nonneutral results. Let us illustrate this. The equalization of interest rates and credit conditions for large and small producers would be considered a neutral policy according to this view. The same would be argued of a policy that equalizes tax rates on unincorporated enterprises and big corporations, of the elimination of preferential subsidies or technical assistance programs for small farmers, and of doing away with price support schemes for independent producers in agriculture and mining.

All of these measures imply a move toward less discriminatory, more uniform market rules. And yet they do not have a neutral distributive effect. Lower productivity sectors like small producers may require discretionary, favorable rules of access to credit and technical assistance or lower taxes to compensate for insufficient land, limited technical knowledge, lower skills, or exploitative intermediaries. This is in the essence of an equity with growth strategy. The alternative, that is, moving toward uniform market rules for these sectors, may in fact force out of business a large segment of the lower productivity producers. This not only has a regressive income effect but also severely aggravates unemployment by weakening one of the most labor-absorptive economic activities.

The argument may be extended to other sectors. Consider liberalization of international capital flows. In theory this is a policy that would benefit all firms equally in the case of high domestic interest rates. In practice, it is only large banks and large business firms that can establish close links with the international capital market and obtain the loans. Middle-size and small enterprises must borrow in the more expensive domestic financial market. Capital flows liberalization results, in practice, in discriminatory treatment of middle and small producers.

Liberalization in the market for agricultural land may imply that poor farmers who had some access to land as a result of land reform will sell land back to previous owners, given the noncompetitive conditions and unequal market power of both groups during a generalized process of market liberalization. Deregulating the use of urban land may favor speculators with advance knowledge and good banking connections rather than low or middle-income families with housing needs. The rules of the market in the provision of education, health, and housing will almost certainly reduce access to lower-income groups, given higher costs and limited purchasing power by these groups.

All the processes that we have described were taking place with different intensity as part of the neoconservative economic program in some countries in Latin America. Most of these policy measures were assumed to enhance competitiveness, equality of access and opportunity, and less discriminatory, discretionary treatment of firms, individuals, or sectors in the economy. Often they reinforced, instead, a bias against lower productivity sectors, smaller firms, and poorer groups.

Other mechanisms through which orthodox monetarism may induce the concentration of income and assets were discussed in Chapters 3 and 7. It was found that concentration took place: (1) if a deliberate policy of privatization of public enterprises is undertaken in such a way that economic conglomerates with an excess of liquid funds are allowed to buy undervalued public assets; (2) if asset redistribution programs like land reform are deliberately reversed, restoring land to expropriated owners; and (3) if financial speculation is allowed to persist for an extended period of several years, during which access to liquid funds is heavily concentrated in a few powerful economic groups.

Let us explore this aspect further. Speculative gains are not equally distributed in the population. They are likely to be higher for those groups with better access to information about policy changes and about probable future movements in relative prices. The advantage is also for those groups that have access to liquidity either from their own financial ventures or because of privileged access to external funds. Why would financial speculation be a result attributed to the orthodox policies? It was argued before that the persistence of stagflation and generalized market disequilibrium, as a result of the policies, provided a fertile ground for capital gains through speculation in various markets, with significant effects on the process of asset concentration.

The conclusion from the previous discussion is obvious. The neutrality claim of monetarism in its Latin American version is indeed a weak one. Empirical evidence shows that stabilization programs were systematically accompanied by nonneutral distributive effects, that is, by income and asset concentration toward high-income groups. We have analyzed the various reasons and mechanisms that produced this result. It turns out that in this approach to stabilization, as in any other, some groups must lose in the process of adjusting the economy to a lower rate of inflation. It is perhaps no coincidence that in the cases we have examined, the main losers were groups considered antagonistic to the political coalition that was presiding over the economic changes, of which the stabilization program was such a key element.

Stabilization Policies and Stagflation

An ex post facto evaluation of the impact of the neoconservative stabilization policies, as we have just done, is not enough to understand *why* specific policy instruments caused a certain effect on inflation, output, and unemployment. Chapters 6 and 7 were devoted to elucidating causal factors and explaining the stagflationary consequences of the policies.

Let us briefly sum up the main points that emerged from that discussion.

As is well known, the conventional orthodox view assumes an economy characterized by homogeneous, atomistic markets, perfect information, and fully flexible prices. A more complex but realistic view of the modern economy would question the homogeneity assumption. Two clearly differentiated segments would be distinguished: one, an administered-price sector that includes manufactures, the public sector, and the labor sector; and a sector consisting of primary producing activities, commerce, and other services.

The administered-price sectors are characterized by pricing mechanisms that are quite unaffected by demand shifts in the short run. Typically, prices are set as a markup over normalized long-term variable costs independent of short-term variations. Wages, a key component of variable costs, are determined as a function of other workers' wages and of expected future inflation. Usually, wage increases are readily transferred to prices through the markup rule that we referred to above.

This price and wage behavior in the administered-price sector is responsible for the observed limited downward flexibility in prices that often afflicts the economies where administered pricing is significant. This is often reinforced by inflationary expectations and by indexation of key prices, which becomes a widely used mechanism to avoid the relative losses from inflation.

The existence of frequent external price shocks in the new international scenario that has prevailed since the early 1970s does nothing but reinforce the importance of supply-side effects behind current inflation. The insistence on one-sided, demand-management policies to deal with this type of inflation lies at the root of persistent inflation and the recessionary tendencies that often go with it.

This happens because monetary and fiscal contraction will be fully effective in reducing prices and wages in the flexible-price sectors, which are not the leading or predominant activities in the price and wage determination process. The effect on the administered-price sectors will be slow and gradual, given external shocks and institutional and structural rigidities that do not allow prices and wages to respond immediately to changes in demand. The adjustment in the fixed-price sectors in the short run will consist in reducing output and employment rather than prices.

How much of this is relevant in the Latin American context? Our review of empirical evidence for some Latin American economies seemed to suggest that it is. Modern sector activities, equivalent to the administered-price segment in industrial economies, determine prices by similar markup rules. Wages are also shown to be largely independent of demand conditions and heavily influenced by expectations of future price increases and by relative wages. However, other input costs seem to be as important as wages as a cost-push factor in the case of Latin American economies: the cost of imported inputs and that of working capital. The first one is affected by exchange rate changes and the second by variations in the rate of interest. Large devaluations and sudden sharp increases in the interest rate due to monetary tightness and financial liberalization were typical components of monetarist stabilization programs. Both had the effect of generating serious cost-push pressures.

On the other hand, exogenous supply shocks are even more important than they are in developed economies. The reason is that in addition to raw materials price increases, chronic imbalances in the external and food-producing sectors tend to result in periodic scarcities of foreign exchange and food supplies, which are eliminated by discrete and sharp increases in prices.

What we have described are significant characteristics of Latin American economies functioning under normal conditions. But authoritarian governments do not generate normal conditions in the economy. Certainly the labor market is not allowed to function normally. Labor organizations are restricted, collective bargaining is eliminated or severely curtailed, and wages are controlled. What this means is that wage-push pressures cannot occupy the central role that they play in price determination in modern economies. Rather, wages play the role of the residual adjustment factor for price stabilization. In fact, real wages fell up to 40% during the orthodox stabilization experiment.

But the fact that wages are controlled does not mean that there are no cost-push pressures in the economy. In the cases that we examined, strong cost-push pressures originated in price deregulation, exchange rate devaluations, and financial sector liberalization. These pressures were perpetuated by strong inflationary expectations and widespread indexation schemes.

If the sequence of various policy actions is followed, a clear picture of the stagflation-inducing factors emerges. At the outset, demand contraction is accompanied by deregulation of prices. Due to previous repressed inflation and high uncertainty, a price explosion follows, validated by indexed key prices. This is the first supply shock. It is followed by others: devaluation, rise in interest rates, and increases in the price of raw materials. Because of the reinforcing nature of all these mechanisms, the supply effect dominates over the contraction in demand. Prices rise and output falls.

What is important to stress once again is that during this phase, prices are not driven up by wages but by the costs of other inputs (raw materials, working capital) and by autonomous price decisions by firms in the administered-price sector, which react by increasing markups when inflationary expectations are a "random walk" because of scarce information and high uncertainty. Firms charge a risk premium that has the effect of driving prices beyond what is justified by existing cost pressures.

In sum, limited downward flexibility in prices and wages in the administered sector of the economy diminish the effectiveness of demand management policies as a stabilization mechanism. Policy-induced supply shocks resulting from price deregulation, external price increases, and devaluation and financial liberalization only compound the problem. The consequence is a long and costly adjustment process in the economy.

Lessons from Experience

What lessons, as far as economic stabilization is concerned, can be learned from our review of theory and experience? Most current views would agree that contemporary inflation is a complex process of interaction among demand, cost, and expectation factors. An approach that ignores some of these factors is likely to result in an unnecessarily long transition period and one that will generate deeper recession and more unemployment than necessary.

What is needed is a comprehensive policy package that takes into account the interdependencies between demand management and those policies oriented to reducing cost pressures and curbing expectations. The right balance has to be struck among these essential elements of an anti-inflationary strategy. The control of money supply and government expenditures does play a role but not a unique one. Supply "disinflationary shocks" may also be necessary, given cost-push and structural factors behind current inflation. Action to reverse expectations through some kind of incomes policy is also a key component of the policy package. It is obvious from recent experience that the failure to deal with this side of the problem has had a lot to do with resilient inflation during the first phases of orthodox stabilization in Latin America.

Intertemporal consistency between different policies seems also to be a critical factor in the success or failure of stabilization programs. This is particularly true when dealing simultaneously with stabilization objectives and structural transformation, as is often the case in Latin America. Wrong timing, lowering tariffs too rapidly, or deregulating external financial flows at an early stage of the stabilization program may imply a high trade-off between policy objectives in the short run. The same will happen if interdependencies in the effects of seemingly unrelated policy measures are not recognized. It was clear in Chapter 7 that it was the accumulated effect of financial liberalization, exchange rate devaluation, and monetary contraction that had such a severe stagflationary effect whereas each of these policies independently considered may have implied a more acceptable trade-off between inflation and unemployment.

Let us now emphasize some specific points concerning each of the components of the anti-inflation strategy. As far as demand management is concerned, it was stressed throughout our analysis that alternative forms of contractionary policies are possible and that the consequences of choosing one rather than another will not be neutral from the point of view of equity. The policy mix between monetary and fiscal contraction is important. Too much reliance on reductions in money supply will push interest rates up. This will have a negative effect on investment but more so in smaller firms since large firms do not depend on borrowing as much as medium-size and small firms do. Relying excessively on public spending cuts, on the other hand, will diminish the provision of essential social services to low-income groups and will worsen the employment situation as a consequence of a lower level of public investment, particularly in labor-intensive construction activities.

Choosing between expenditure cuts and taxation is another critical aspect of stabilization policy. If direct taxes can be increased, this will be better from a distributive point of view than raising (regressive) indirect taxes or decreasing expenditures. This choice is important because through an adequate management of the composition of taxes and expenditures at least part of the regressive impact of the stabilization program may be checked.

The other critical lesson from experience vis-à-vis demand management policies is that not only its distributive impact must be taken into account but also the effectiveness of monetary management has to increase. Developing new instruments that allow for a more extended role for open market operations on the part of the government is part of the solution and one that would help in sterilizing unprogramed expansions in the monetary base. On the other hand, a more homogeneous, less segmented financial market would contribute to an increase in the effectiveness of monetary instruments.

As a second major component, we have stressed the importance of supply factors behind inflation. What are the policies best suited to deal with inflationary pressures that have a strong causal factor in the supply side? We already know what the Latin American structuralist reply of the 1950s and 1960s was: we have to eliminate supply bottlenecks. Since this may require a very significant reallocation of investment resources, the approach to stabilization must necessarily be gradual and rather long term. Bottlenecks, be they sources of energy, other intermediate inputs, food products, or foreign exchange, will not disappear in the short period of time for which stabilization programs are usually designed.

In the short run, cost-push pressures can be neutralized by applying supply "disinflationary shocks." The most common suggestion in the past has been to reduce the cost of labor. This can be done, as in the Latin American orthodox policies, by outright reductions in real wages or elimination of the minimum wage, or both. It is not irrelevant to stress that this policy has been viable for more than very short periods of time only in the presence of authoritarian governments that have eliminated labor legislation, outlawed labor organizations, and been extremely repressive toward labor in general. The reason is obvious: the negative income distribution effect may be dramatic, as has been shown. Other possibilities, like reducing indirect taxes while increasing direct taxation, reducing social security contributions, etc., must be examined carefully for their distributive impact.

Supply policies are by nature sectoral rather than aggregate, across-the-board policies. They must focus on eliminating particular bottlenecks. An energy program, a food self-reliance program, or a selective export promotion program is the type of action required to deal with structural problems on the supply side. These actions are of necessity discretionary and selective. They require concerted action by the government and the private sector and a concentration of resources in a few high-priority activities. These kinds of selective policies are different from the orthodox approach that seeks to homogenize through the market the treatment given to all sectors and factors of production.

Cost reduction and increased availability of key, scarce inputs is but one side of supply-management policies. The other is that of stimulating productivity. This is particularly relevant for an approach that wishes to avoid the frequently observed pattern where adjustment costs end up falling mostly on labor through drastic reductions in real wages. How can the adjustment burden on labor be alleviated? The more labor productivity grows, the less real wage reductions will be required to bring inflation under control. Policies directed to stimulating productivity growth will be more effective when inflation is at a moderate level. At very high rates, gains in productivity will be of little importance given the much larger relative magnitude of macroeconomic disequilibrium.

A third element in a comprehensive stabilization program is incomes policy. As inflation has become a more persistent phenomenon, inflationary expectations play a larger role in maintaining an upward trend in the price level. For expectations to be reversed, some future course for prices and wages has to be imposed or agreed upon.

An important factor to be present in a successful incomes policy is the explicit recognition of how the relative positions of the different economic agents may change as a result of the policy. This is not only important in terms of labor and profit shares but also within the labor sector. Relative wages and "wage contours" seem to be significant factors determining workers' behavior during a stabilization program. If some workers feel that they are paying a higher cost than others, this will result in pressures for relative wage increases that will almost certainly be followed by other workers' demanding higher wages. An agreed-upon relative wage structure performs the useful function of stabilizing the wage drift factor that gradually but increasingly weakens the effectiveness of incomes policy. In this respect, a stabilization program that increases wage differentials, as many orthodox programs have, while providing the right incentives for higher productivity in the more skilled faction of the labor force may at the same time seriously undermine attempts at enforcing any kind of incomes policy.

A final lesson to be learned from neoconservative experiments in Latin America is that economic stabilization cannot be separated from long-term changes and policies. These are influenced by ideologies, coalitions in power, and the nature of the political regime. All of these are major forces interfering with "pure," rational, technical policies. As with all areas of human endeavor, economic choices are not made in a vacuum, not even under authoritarian regimes that live under the delusion that these variables are under control. They may well be for a while, but sooner or later these other forces will make their presence felt and will affect the course of whichever policies are being implemented.

The long-term neoconservative project consists in organizing the economy and society under free market principles. In its Latin American version, fragile market mechanisms seem to need—according to its advocates—the protection of an authoritarian government that, in the process, disposes of most individual rights, except for the unrelenting pursuit of economic freedom, which the authoritarian regime seeks to guarantee.

Will these kind of policies restore the social consensus that broke apart during the last phases of popular-socialist experiments in Latin America? One can only guess. Although neoconservative policies can exhibit some success in checking inflation and balance of payments problems, they have also generated a significant increase in inequalities within the economy and society. The system supports itself in the continuous and persistent use of force. This cannot but build enormous tensions.

Thus, again, the problem to be solved is not a technical one, although past lessons must be learned about the need to "defer to normal economic constraints" and to recognize the high social and political cost associated with economic inefficiency. The main problem consists in restoring some degree of consensus about basic issues: growth and distribution, the role of the various economic agents (business, labor, government), rules of the economic game, and the political system that supports a civilized interaction among the members of society.

If the political system is going to be a democratic one, economic policies must necessarily be a reflection of a basic underlying consensus. For these policies to have a chance, they cannot persistently generate increasing inequalities, nor can they systematically exclude significant sectors of society, as neoconservative policies in Latin America so often have. On the other hand, they must prove that efficiency is not in contradiction with continued progress toward a more egalitarian society.

Index

Adjustment processes:
deregulation of financial
markets, 163–171;
deregulation of prices,
158–163; of economic
stabilization, 149–183;
external shocks and
devaluation, 171–175; fiscal
adjustment, 155–158;
liberalization of external
capital flows, 178–183;
monetary control, 151–154;
tariff reduction, 175–178
Administered-price sectors,
198–199
Agrarian reform in Chile, 63,
67, 82
Agricultural sector: change in
production composition and
employment, 77–78;
privatization and, 67
Allende administration, 63
Andean Pact, 58
Anti-inflation phase, of
stabilization, 58–59
Argentina: authoritarianism in,
19; economic deterioration in
1970s, 29; export expansion,
36; financial reform program,
164–165; monetarist
programs, 13; in the 1960s,
19, 22, 23; open economy

monetarism in, 116–118;
tariff reduction, 176
Authoritarian government:
economic conditions and, 200;
and orthodox economic
policies, 16, 18
Authoritarianism, origins of,
19–20
Automatic adjustment, 90; of
exchange rate, 60

Balance of payments, 21, 59;
deficit, 31, 56; disequilibrium,
171; during Chilean
experiment, 42, 53, 57;
monetary approach to, 115;
United States problems, 34
Bank failures in Chile, 61
Bankruptcies, 32; in Chile, 61
Bolivia, monetarist programs, 13
Borrowing, cost of, 165–166,
169–170
Brazil, 23–28; authoritarianism
in, 19; export expansion, 36;
foreign trade, 25; in the 1960s,
22, 23; orthodoxy of
economic policies, 23–28;
public investment, 26–28
Built-in indexing, 114
Business sector, effects of open
economy on, 80

207

Designer: Wolfgang Lederer
Compositor: Innovative Media Inc.
Text: 10/13 Sabon
Display: Melior
Printer: Vail-Ballou Press
Binder: Vail-Ballou Press